EssaySnark's Strategies for the
2014-'15 MBA Application for
THE WHARTON SCHOOL

EssaySnark's Strategies for the 2014-'15 MBA Application for THE WHARTON SCHOOL

by EssaySnark®

Snarkolicious Press

First published September 13, 2012
Current edition first published June 12, 2014, updated November 1, 2014
version 4.1

Snarkolicious Press
P. O. Box 50021
Palo Alto, CA 94303

www.snarkoliciouspress.com

978 1 938098 24 6

© 2011-2014 by EssaySnark

Cover image © Eric Isselée, used under license from Fotolia.com

All rights reserved. No part of this book may be reproduced or transmitted in any form or by any means, electronic or mechanical, including photocopying, recording, or by an information storage system, without permission from the publisher. Essay questions reproduced within are copyright Wharton School of Business.

This publication is provided "as is", without warranty of any kind, either express or implied. The author and Snarkolicious Press assume no liability for errors or omissions in this publication or other documents which are referenced or linked to this publication. While we certainly hope that you will be successful in your quest for admission to an MBA program, we cannot offer any promises that you will be, whether or not you adopt the advice provided herein. In no event shall Snarkolicious Press or its authors, principals, subsidiaries, partners, or owners, be liable for any special, incidental, indirect or consequential damages of any kind, or any damages whatsoever, arising out of or in conjunction with the use or performance of this information. Applicants to any graduate program or university should verify the school's policies, application requirements, processes, procedures, and other criteria. This publication could include technical or other inaccuracies or typographical errors. Changes are periodically added to the information herein; these changes will be incorporated into new editions of this publication. Thus, different versions or formats of this publication may include different information.

Look for other *SnarkStrategies Guides* (digital and paperback) at your favorite bookseller or on the EssaySnark blahg at http://essaysnark.com.

Follow EssaySnark on Twitter!

"The simpler it is, the better I like it."

Peter Lynch, Wharton '68

About this *SnarkStrategies Guide*

You may not know it based on looking at the essay questions but there are many changes afoot at Wharton and this *SnarkStrategies Guide* is the best resource for reading the tea leaves. We offer tips and tricks on how to approach the application, though of course, if you've read any of the other *SnarkStrategies Guides* then you know already where we draw the line: EssaySnark will not be telling you what to write in your essays.

Ours is the DIY "teach you to fish" approach. You're going to have to hit the pavement and (hopefully) visit the school and do your own first-hand research, along with using this spiffy essay guide, in order to be fully equipped for success with your Wharton application.

If you find yourself stuck at any point, drop on over to http://essaysnark.com and explore the resources we have available, or email gethelpnow@essaysnark.com and we'll see what we can do to assist.

Table of Contents

About this SnarkStrategies Guide...1
What's Changing at Wharton..1
    Wharton's priorities...3
        Wharton and Harvard..4
        Wharton and innovation..5
        Knowledge for Action..6
    Wharton's strengths..7
    What the new admissions team has done..9
    An open secret...11
Timing: Which Round?...14
Traits of a Wharton Admit..16
Your Wharton Application Strategy..22
    What to do when..22
    The 5 key points of a Wharton "gain" essay...23
    What do they mean by "substance"?...24
    Career Goals..25
The Wharton Essay: What You Will Gain (aka Professional Objectives)...............33
    What needs to go in this main essay?...34
    Wharton and You..36
        A common mistake: Not sharing enough of yourself....................................37
    A very important suggestion...39
    What to include in your "Why Wharton" content..40
    Can I re-use my Wharton essay for Harvard?...41
    Can I re-use my Harvard essay for Wharton?...42
    Can I re-use my Wharton essay for Stanford? 42
    Can I re-use my Wharton essay for Columbia?..42
    The schools know that your goals may change..44
The Optional Essays..45
Reapplicant Essay..49
The Wharton/Lauder Joint Degree..51
The Wharton Team-Based Discussion and Your Interview..54
    Where are interviews held...55
    How it works...56
    How to prepare...58
What to Do Next..61

What's Changing at Wharton

At first glance, it may seem like the answer to that is, "Nothing much." Partly this is because Wharton has been, well, kinda stagnant.

For 2014, they haven't even changed their essays, really; all they did was tweak one single word in the first question, and drop the second one.

That can hardly be seen as earth-shaking.

Or can it?

Wharton is clearly following Harvard's lead, in going down to a single essay.

Note to the adcoms: The schools that have such limited questions tend to be seen less favorably by applicants, in terms of the "getting to know you" process. Yeah, it may seem like less work for the candidate upfront, but in the end, applicants usually feel that they weren't able to share enough with the school. But that's a separate conversation. To you the applicant: Expect to feel challenged and frustrated by what you are allowed to convey in the single essay. We'll cover lots and lots of strategies and recommendations for literally how to approach this limitation as we move through this guide.

Back to earth-shaking (or not): Wharton has never before kept any essay question the same from year to year. They have always revamped all essays fairly dramatically every single season. So this year is different.

In the past, the Wharton essay questions were also often quite difficult; many applicants had trouble even understanding what the school was asking. A difficult-worded question makes for some not-great essays. We're very pleased to see that they've abandoned those types of questions in the last two years. This year, the single question is phrased well enough. What will you gain from the MBA? Or another way to put it: Why do you want to go to Wharton?

The changes — or more precisely, the lack thereof — says that it's status quo no longer at Wharton.

Wharton has a new dean coming in this summer, and we believe that the Board of Overseers selected him as someone to advance the priorities that they quietly defined for themselves some years back. We believe the main priority they set was to unseat Harvard, and to take Wharton into the next century. (Meaning, the 21st one. As in, the one we're currently living in today. Wharton has seem a little stuck.)

Wharton as a brand is stable and conservative and solid. However, we don't know anyone who sees Wharton as thought leader. Wharton just doesn't come to mind when we think of "cutting edge." Sure, Wharton professors are quoted in the media frequently, and definitely this is a respected brand. We don't think that's going to change. It's just not a school that — prior to now — has struck us as altogether hungry.

We've been pretty unimpressed with Dean Robertson, frankly, and it's probably time for him to move on. He's seemed rather checked out lately, and our impression is that Wharton got a little lazy. That old "resting on its laurels" thing. They were touting innovation as a big byword a few years ago – there was even an essay question about it – yet we just don't see all that much in the way of newness or transformation coming out of Philadelphia. It's like they hit their heyday with the new building about ten years ago, and made some changes to the curriculum and lifelong learning along the way, but those things just brought them in line with what other schools like Booth and Haas were already doing.

Wharton's reputation has also suffered blows over the past decade from a few misdeeds.

Yes, misdeeds. Oh, you hadn't heard?

For example, there was the 2008 ethics scandal in its admissions department: the head of admissions was working as an admissions consultant. Definitely a conflict of interest. In 2011 and 2012, the school was embarrassed by an insider trading scandal featuring three members of the Wharton Class of 1983. Certainly the ISB was even more humiliated by that, since its *founder* is now in jail as a result.

This one isn't a "misdeed" but, in summer 2011, an assessment from *Poets&Quants* determined that a huge percentage of admitted Wharton students come from a very short list of Ivy League colleges and premier companies like McKinsey. The implicit accusation in that article was that Wharton is elitist. That certainly works against the school's efforts to claim that they're open to all, and that everyone has an equal opportunity of getting in.

Then most recently, the Wall Street Journal published a piece titled "What's Wrong with Wharton?" (9/27/13). Soon after, Admissions Director Ankur Kumar announced she was leaving, quite unexpectedly and with no fanfare, and with no cush new job lined up. We believe that having *two* waves of negative press was her undoing in the role.

Of course, none of Wharton's breaches is quite as bad as the atrocious interview with Columbia's Dean Hubbard in the movie *Inside Job*... which EssaySnark believes was responsible for the massive drop in applications at Columbia during the 2011-'12 admissions season. Wharton also saw a dip that year but nothing like Columbia suffered.

As a school, Wharton has buffed up its curricular content on ethics in business, and they are certainly going to be sensitive to any perceived breach of ethics in your application. Don't be tempted to lie or fudge the truth. Wharton and many other schools now enlist third-party organizations for background checks of all accepted candidates. You wouldn't want to lose your golden ticket at the last minute because they uncovered some half-truths or misrepresentations in your application.

So Wharton Admissions is under new management, and they have a new dean coming in. We believe this *change-that's-no-change* on the MBA application is a sign of the changing of the guard.

Wharton's priorities

It typically takes about two or three years before a change of leadership starts to make a visible difference at a school, so it's not like you will necessarily expect to see anything new right away. Dean Garrett isn't even there yet. If you're in the next Wharton class, then you can expect to see some announcements coming that may affect you – but that's going to be quite aways off from today.

We believe that Dean Garrett was selected because the Board of Trustees sees him as the right person to execute on the vision that they have already defined; we don't predict that Garrett is necessarily going to bring new ideas. We weren't privy to the conversations but we believe that his marching orders are simply to unseat Harvard.

The initiatives that the Board of Trustees has hinted at publicly as important are international connections, and distance learning/online education. Garrett is known for embracing technology in education and he obviously has an international profile, coming from Australia (he also spent many years at Southern California universities like USC, as well as teaching at Wharton many years ago).

So that you can get a sense for what's going on at the school, these are EssaySnark prognostications of what's going on behind the scenes at Wharton today:

1. We believe the simplified Wharton application reflects one of their internal organizational priorities and *that Wharton is going to go full force after Harvard in an attempt to re-establish itself as a leader in the space.* This matters to you as an applicant.

2. We also understand that Wharton has had an emphasis on innovation in the curriculum, which has been ongoing for a couple years now. This does not impact you as an applicant – unless you have something in your background and/or your future goals that is in that domain, in which case it would be wise to talk that up in your essay.

3. We know that the new dean will be focusing on international opportunities and global relationships. This might matter to you as an applicant, depending on your profile and most importantly, your goals.

4. Presumably as part of their effort to modernize and to get there before Harvard does, Wharton has now embraced the MOOC movement (massively open online courses) and is a major contributor to Coursera. They are also pushing the "flipped classroom" which is a term that speaks to a trend in education whereby students get access to a course portal where they study the materials in advance or even watch pre-recorded lectures from the professor, and then spend the time in class to take the discussion to the next level – far beyond what a traditional course structure can do. Wharton is moving aggressively to put content online both for the public and

also for students. They have pre-term math courses available in the summertime for the incoming class this fall. This new emphasis honestly doesn't matter to you as an applicant unless you're somehow interested in the field of education as your MBA focus. We can see people tossing out mentions of Wharton and Coursera in an essay and in most cases we'd probably call that "essay-stuffing" – meaning, making random references that aren't well integrated or meaningful to the applicant. So be conservative on how you might use the bright ideas you get from reading about this stuff here in this guide.

5. Wharton is continuing to seek to expand its reputation beyond being "a finance school" - particularly in the wake of that Wall Street Journal article. But it doesn't take any type of crystal ball to predict that; it's pretty obvious that's what they're doing, with broader emphasis on entrepreneurship and healthcare, and more niche features like analytics and social venture. They've had these strengths going for them already, but they aren't necessarily known for them to the extent that we think they want to be. Expect increased messaging around these non-finance disciplines. This doesn't really matter to you as an applicant in terms of affecting your chances for admission, though of course it does in terms of showing fit to the school and understanding what they're about (and expressing that appropriately in the app).

To give you some insight into our thought processes behind these stated priorities – remember, we're no Wharton insiders, this is us being analysts of the admissions landscape and speaking to the schools as admissions consultants, it's not based on some direct access to the secret workings of the school – why do we believe that Wharton switched gears internally to focus on rankings and specifically put Harvard in its sights awhile ago?

Wharton and Harvard

Well, the Wharton Class of 2015 had a whopping 725 average GMAT score – higher than almost any other school.

Most of you already know that a school's average GMAT score affects its placement in most of the rankings. This provides a perverse incentive to the schools to admit those with very high scores. Sure, someone with a high score has demonstrated that they know how to study; you're not going to do well on the GMAT without that. And students who study are better students. But the GMAT is just one datapoint, and making admissions decisions with an overfocus on the test can result in some unintended consequences. A case study in another way to do admissions is Duke Fuqua, whose admissions team doesn't discount the GMAT but they definitely are not running their admissions team to maximize the average student score.

The advantage that Wharton has – and that you have – is that they have a huge class to fill. They can get that mean GMAT to stay stable by admitting some crazy-scoring finance or consulting or international applicants who present the 780s and the 790s and the occasional perfect 800, while still easily accommodating a whole slew of 660s and the like. You're totally not doomed at Wharton if you have a low(er) score. But the score does matter, which we go into detail about starting on page 16.

The reason we make this claim about Wharton gunning for Harvard is because the year-before Wharton average GMAT was 718. Going from 718 to 725 is HUGE. That change does not happen by accident. No school ends up with a stratospheric average GMAT at random, and they DEFINITELY don't see such a severe YoY change except by design.

Even more noteworthy? Their full GMAT range for all students for the Class of 2015 was 630 to 790.

That is, the LOWEST score they accepted was a 630.

That is really high for a lowest score at a top school.

(That reminds us of a trivia question: Which state in the U.S. has the lowest highest point? You know, the highest point in the state is lower than any other state. Well, which do you think? We'll tell you at the end of this chapter.)

By comparison, Harvard has lowest scores that dip down to like 550 or so. That's a dramatic difference.

Wharton carefully crafted their class in order to end up at that level. We don't know what the average GMAT will be for the Class of 2016 (as of this writing, those students haven't even arrived on campus) however we're guessing that it will be comparable.

Wharton has been tied for #1 (with Harvard and Stanford) on the U.S. News list of the best bschools, and certainly they remain popular among Brave Supplicants everywhere. After all, who wouldn't want to go to Wharton?!? (That is, if you weren't accepted to Harvard.) However, that's just one list. Wharton hasn't been at the top of the BusinessWeek rankings since the year 2000, at which time Kellogg bumped them out. (Kellogg? Yes, Kellogg. Another school that has ceased to impress us.) In the 2012 BW rankings, Wharton came out #4, and we predict that the 2014 BW list will move them further down – still Top 10, but definitely not closer to the top. Those rankings are typically published in November so we'll have to wait and see.

EssaySnark has been watching, and we just haven't seen Wharton do anything special of late.

This school just hasn't been acting hungry. It doesn't seem nimble, or agile, to use the trendy term. It's been relying on its own long-standing reputation and coasting a bit.

Wharton and innovation

Wharton has been on an innovation kick lately – at least, they've been focusing on it in the past few years in admissions, and we were seeing them talking it up through about a year ago. It was in a lot of their messaging. That's subsided a bit but we don't believe that there's less focus on it within the school. And despite the public language, we never actually see the school itself doing much innovating. They launched a new research center around innovation a couple years back and put some resources there, so maybe it's just a matter of time. Professor Ulrich, who leads the innovation research center, was heavily involved in some of the changes to the admissions processes around the Team-Based Discussion, and he has frequently led those sessions with applicants himself. But in terms of the curriculum and coursework? Wharton seems to be what we call a "fast follower" (sometimes not so fast); they mostly have trotted out changes on a lag to what their peers do.

Here's an example:

Wharton re-branded itself a few years back, and they now have a very nice promise to alumni to provide a certain amount of education throughout the rest of your life after you graduate. They overhauled the curriculum and the changes were fully rolled out for the class entering in 2012 – but at that point, the curriculum wasn't "new" (they announced it way back in 2010) and the changes they made weren't so revolutionary.

The main way they changed it is to make the first year a lot more flexible, with the core curriculum changeable based on your background, experience, and interests. In fact, you can choose to spread the core requirements out over your entire two years instead of cramming all of them into the first two semesters. Other schools, specifically Booth, Stanford, Haas, and Yale, all have some of these elements that Wharton has adapted; Haas rolled these changes out in 2004, so if you're talking about innovation…

If you discuss the curriculum in your Wharton essays – which you might want to do, given that they've specifically asked about what you want from the MBA – EssaySnark would avoid calling it "new" since it's now been around awhile (even though they still call it "the new curriculum" on their website).

Knowledge for Action

That 2012 Wharton rebranding campaign that we mentioned centered around a tagline of "Knowledge for Action."

This reminds us of Columbia's emphasis on "theory and practice" in the late 2000s. It was really important to the school at the time, but now where is it? Sometimes it comes up as an afterthought in an info session presentation, but it's largely absent from the conversation. Same with Wharton and this branding.

Wharton had an essay question two years ago asking candidates to talk about a time when they put knowledge into action. Thankfully, they've abandoned that, as it was often difficult for people to do a good job with it. Now we don't see this "knowledge for action" tagline hardly anywhere on the Wharton site (you can find it tucked away at the very bottom right corner). They have a page featuring media coverage on it where the last entry was from April 2012. They had another page with some Storify content that now fails to load. Wonder how much they paid to branding consultants to come up with that dud?

Wharton's strengths

Before we get accused of Wharton-bashing, we do have respect for what the school offers. It's a top-notch education (with the price tag to go along with that). It's easy to see why you're interested in this school. The word "Wharton" is usually spoken in the same breath as "Harvard" and "Stanford." Wharton certainly has the name recognition, global reputation, and brand awareness to make it a popular place for BSers to target. International applicants remain especially keen on Wharton.

They're more than a finance school, and the assessment in the fall 2013 WSJ article was that it was their slow response to the changing dynamics of bschool applicants and recruiters that had caused their drop in apps. While it's true that in the post-2008 crash MBA frenzy, Wharton saw 7,500 apps, and the most recent classes have seen ~1,500 fewer... 6,000 apps is still a lot.

Wharton is trying to showcase their identity as being beyond finance, however in their favor we want to point out that they were actually one of the most responsive schools during the 2008 economic crisis, much more so than other schools we saw. Wharton actively adjusted their classroom experience to incorporate and react to the events that were unfolding in real time around all of us. Other schools seemed caught in the headlights and – except for NYU with their rockstar Professor Roubini – weren't very fleet of foot in that time.

At Wharton, there are top-notch teachers, in finance and across the departments of the school. They have a very nice facility. Philadelphia is a great town (though it wasn't always considered the safest; this is improving). Wharton only accepts high-quality students. There's a lot going for you if you get in.

Wharton remains one of the top sources for high-end recruiting into consulting firms and to Wall Street – you can't go wrong with Wharton if that's the type of environment you're targeting. Their MBA education is rigorous, and valuable. If you want to go into finance, or you have an international career in mind, or if you're interested in social venture, real estate, or certain forms of entrepreneurship (products and services especially; perhaps not tech/software), Wharton is an obvious choice.

And, with their large entering classes, it's often fairly straightforward for the stronger candidates to get an offer. There's a lot of supply available to meet the demand.

If you can't make it into Harvard – and you're that caliber of applicant – then you can easily find a spot at Wharton. Many Brave Supplicants we know are able to pull this off. It's in all honesty a much easier proposition than trying to break into HBS or Stanford. You won't be waltzing into Wharton, but if you do your homework and you are an above-average candidate in at least a couple areas, it's pretty easy to convince the adcom that you belong there.

Which is kind of our point.

It's MUCH easier to get into Wharton today than it is to get into Harvard.

It didn't used to be that way. Five or ten years ago, if you got into Wharton, you almost undoubtedly also got into Harvard – and sometimes people chose Philly over Boston. That choice is almost unheard of today. One admissions consultant was even quoted as saying that he had a client who was offered a $70k scholarship to Wharton and still chose HBS.

Even more telling? We had clients choose Booth over Wharton. **Granted, Booth was offering a sweet scholarship in most of those cases, but still. (And yes, it surprised us; we have a hard time buying the argument that Booth is better than Wharton.) This truly speaks to the individual factors that go into the bschool decision, yet it also surely underscores this idea that Wharton lately has not been quite what it once was.** For the record, we've never, ever heard of someone going to Booth instead of to Harvard or Stanford.

So all of our warnings and assessment about how Wharton got soft is based on how we've seen the admissions landscape change over many years, and it's in how we've watched the school react publicly (or not) to the changes in the bschool marketplace.

We do think that change is happening there NOW. And we do expect the admissions process to become more competitive at Wharton – maybe not this year, but certainly a tightening of standards is happening, and we will watch to see how this coming admissions season plays out.

All of this backstory is just to state the case that:

1. If your profile is strong, you totally have a chance here, and
2. The Wharton adcom will be crafting an incoming class that is competitive to Harvard's.

Not everyone can go to Harvard, so Wharton will be picking up the slack – but they're also likely to try and fight harder for the superstar candidates that they decide they really want. Those offers of scholarship money? Expect to see more of them, for potentially higher amounts, for the most impressive candidates.

In the past, as a general rule, Wharton had been kinda stingy when it comes to offering free money. They do make awards of fellowships and they have lots of different categories that they'll consider admitted students for. What we often see though is this: Another program admits the BSer with an offer of funding, and he's also admitted to Wharton, but without any scholarship. We've never seen it work out where Wharton will match the other school. You can ask them to, but we have low confidence they'll decide to throw any bones your direction. If you're applying to Wharton as a "typical" candidate, you should simply recognize the incredible value of the Wharton MBA and be prepared to pay full price for the opportunity. If you end up with some fellowship money, then that will be a bonus. Don't go into the application expecting to get an award; that's not how these decisions should be calculated.

So what will impress Wharton? This strategy guide is written to help you figure that out. But first, let's talk about more changes we've observed.

What the new admissions team has done

We'll leave it to you to evaluate whether these are positives or negatives or a mix of both.

- They (finally!) got a new website in August 2013. This happened under Ankur's leadership, not Maryellen's, but it's still worth noting. You probably never saw, or can't remember, the old website, but we'll tell you it was pretty bad. For a school touting innovation and trying to showcase its modernity, this was pretty late in the game. Columbia only unveiled a new website in the same timeframe so you can see how these schools are again similar.

- They started using their blog a lot more and being much more broad in their messaging, posting articles from different admissions personnel on topics like the surrounding Philadelphia community, on-campus conferences, and other initiatives like the Lauder program. They also expanded the presence on the blog from just the generic "Notes from the Director" which was how Ankur posted news about admissions, to having a more personable (sometimes even folksy) feel with individual posts from actual people. When Maryellen first took over, we started to see posts with more frequency. As the admissions season has gotten underway those are decreasing to only a few posts per month. You can go here for the latest: http://mbablog.wharton.upenn.edu/mba-blog

- They started offering admissions webinars on a variety of subjects though this too has petered out somewhat after an initial push. This is very positive and we wish that all schools would do so. Many schools do online chats but the webinar format is great, particularly when you get an opportunity for Q&A at the end, and the whole thing is recorded. You can find them here: http://mbablog.wharton.upenn.edu/events

- They began industry-specific recruiting events in different cities, like Health Care in Boston and Entrepreneurship in San Francisco. This is sort of a no-brainer, if you ask us, but the way they announced it made it sound like it was this great new novel idea. Yes we're a little jaded. It's great that they're doing these but at the same time, this isn't such an earth-shattering innovation.

- They put a similar new emphasis on different subpopulations in admissions: Diversity Events, Women Events, Military Events, Partner Events. They've always had these, but it appears that there's a greater push of late to be more present with them. Note that Wharton is not a member of The Consortium, which is an organization dedicated to increasing the presence of underrepresented minorities in business, in part by supporting them in pursuing the MBA. Lots of other top schools are also not members, but the ones that are seem to us to be putting a little more muscle behind their claims of increasing diversity. Related to that: Wharton is a member of the Forte Foundation, which is about increasing the number of women in top management positions, and Wharton has shown remarkable progress with the percentage of women in each MBA class, as discussed in this guide.

- They *took down* their so-called Student-to-Student (or "S2S") online discussion forums, with no announcement or fanfare. Admittedly, these were hardly of much use; we only saw like two students EVER participating in them, and one of those two offered some really lame advice. However, this was perhaps the only school that had anything like that, and it was definitely a resource that we told people to use. The forums were completely unmoderated by admissions themselves, and the students who participated were not part of the admissions process, so the quality of the responses was quite variable – but it was a resource. The fact that they never even mentioned anything about closing it, but just closed it, is kind of disturbing. Doesn't that say something about being an open community (or not)?

- They changed their essays fairly radically this year, going down to a single required essay (500 words), and implementing a very confusing two optional essays. The maximum length for the required essays – errr, *essay* – this year is just 500 words. Last year applicants had to write 1,250 words. That's a pretty big change. Of course, you have 1,150 words total available to you this year, when you count the two optional essays – but you shouldn't plan to write any optional essay just because it's available. See page 45 for a complete discussion.

- They formalized a "conditional acceptance" policy which some other schools have but don't publicize. The way this works is Wharton will accept you but only if you improve your profile in some way, typically through a GMAT retake to get your score up. If you don't, then your offer is off the table. This is yet more proof that they're emphasizing high GMAT scores as part of their criteria.

- They also brought their policy on age of GMAT scores in line with what other schools have. The loose rule in bschool admissions is that GMAT scores are good for five years, but how those "five years" are calculated has varied from school to school. Previously at Wharton, your score had to be valid at the time of application submission, which could be almost a year before starting class (so, to apply in Fall 2013, in order to matriculate in Fall 2014, you would've needed to present a test score taken no earlier than August 1, 2009, whereas schools like Harvard accepted scores from 2008). Wharton's policy had excluded some candidates who had the foresight to take the GMAT while still in college and were now, after working for four years, interested in applying. Starting this year, scores must be from tests taken within a roughly 5½ year window (see the Wharton site for exact dates), which is more accommodating of older tests and maps more closely to Harvard.

- Wharton has collaborated with a bunch of other top schools this year to streamline their letters of recommendation. Now Wharton is asking recommenders to answer just two questions, and those questions are identical to what Harvard, Stanford, Yale, Columbia, and a number of other schools are asking. This is mostly a positive change, though it also means you have even less space overall to tell your story – and not every school with standardized recommendation questions actually has standardized recommendation questions. Wharton's are identical to Stanford and Harvard but not necessarily identical to the others.

The key change at The Wharton School itself that we want to mention is their new San Francisco initiative, where about 70 full-time MBA students can study for a semester at their Bay Area campus. Wharton San Francisco moved into new digs about a year ago and the larger facility has more space; it used to be an EMBA-only campus. Not surprisingly, almost all the students who do the San Francisco semester are entrepreneurs. We understand that it's an application-based opportunity and it's becoming quite popular. This isn't something that came out of their admissions team, but it's obviously worth mentioning, in case you want to research this further (and potentially talk about it in your application).

The other main improvement in terms of the student experience at Wharton is that last year, they launched a new class scheduling system which was even written up in BusinessWeek. It's supposed to be infinitely better than the previous points bidding system, Chicago and other schools still use a points system and we've heard real complaints from students about how awful those can be; nobody gets the classes they want, everything is crazy and chaotic and very stressful, and many people end up feeling dissatisfied. Wharton's Course Match system is supposed to be more efficient than the auction system and we hear that everyone is happier because of it.

An open secret

A quick heads-up on some seemingly obvious advice that we need to offer directly since it is apparently often overlooked:

The Wharton website is – as all bschool websites are – a treasure trove of information, hints, guidance, and secret tips, all hidden in broad daylight.

Your first assignment before even thinking about what you might want to write in your Wharton essay is to *study the website.* Study it carefully. Read it word for word.

All that marketing language? Sure, it sounds an awful lot like all the other top schools' websites. Yes, to some degree, it's just fluffy. But at the same time: The adcom wrote the Admissions pages. If you're trying to read the tea leaves about what an adcom wants, this is the best place to start.

To wit, on the first page of the Admissions section[1], we get this:

> **Wharton admissions is all about the right fit and our goal is to give you the information you need to make an informed choice. We want to help you figure out if Wharton is the right place for your background, career goals, learning style, and personal interests.**

Let's dissect that, shall we? The part about your *background, career goals, learning style, and personal interest* in particular.

Don't you think that perhaps the adcom is signaling there that that's what *they* are looking for, when determining if you're a good fit for them?

EssaySnark thinks so. EssaySnark suggests that those are the key criteria that you need to be focusing on as you develop your materials for The Wharton School. After all, how else can you tell them what you hope to "gain" if you don't express it in terms of how it's the right place for you?

Quick warning: Please do NOT crib website marketing copy into your admissions essays! Often the people reading your essays are the ones who *wrote that copy*. They will recognize their words. It will not look good to plagiarize them (no, it won't make it seem like you're all the more motivated and are the "perfect fit" just because you use their language).

The other important nugget of advice that Wharton themselves is serving up to you, completely for free?[2] This:

> **A successful application combines substance, presentation, and good timing.**

They're laying it out directly for you. In fact, that entire page of *Preparing a Successful Application* has oodles of goodies that hopefully you're already well familiar with – you need to study this stuff!

Every school's website is chock full o' useful tidbits like that. We've pulled out just two examples, and already you have a leg up:

1. You know about the criteria the adcom will be using to evaluate your fit to The Wharton School, and
2. You know about the advantage of applying early.

These priceless tips are right there, out in the open, within the front pages of the website.

---

1 http://www.wharton.upenn.edu/mba/admissions/index.cfm as of June 11, 2014
2 http://www.wharton.upenn.edu/mba/admissions/preparing-successful-application.cfm as of June 11, 2014

Most people breeze through them, hunting just for essay questions and deadline dates, and overlooking the wealth of information that the school is providing for free.

Let's break that one sentence down for you to illustrate:

- **Substance:** Your essays must convey who you are and what you want to do with your life, in as much detail as humanly possible within the confines of their limited essay allocations. The bulk of this strategy guide is geared to helping you with the *substance* part.

- **Presentation:** We mentioned this a moment ago and this is what we were talking about. Your written materials need to be complete yet concise; no spelling errors; the appropriate amount of detail; all content relevant to the exercise of positioning your best self in a *professional* fashion. Then, when they invite you to interview, you'll present as a polished and mature individual who's ready for the big leagues. Presentation counts.

- **Good timing:** This means, apply early! Wharton has language on their website (new last year) to encourage applications to come in before the deadline. They also are quite clear that for almost all classes of candidate, you need to apply in Rounds 1 or 2 (not Round 3) – and for reapplicants, EssaySnark strongly recommends a Round 1 app (the reapplicant essay is touched on starting on page 49).

The state with the lowest highest point is Delaware. You probably guessed Florida, didn't you? OK, now we can move on.

Timing: Which Round?

On timing, if you're reading this and considering a Round 3 application to Wharton or anywhere else, you'd better have a good reason for trying so late, and your application better be pretty darn impressive. Most people won't get in with a Round 3 app. You'd be better off waiting just a few short months and trying for the next season's Round 1 in October.

In fact, if you do so, then not only will you be moving yourself out of the LEAST POSSIBLE category of candidate (those applying in Round 3), you'd be moving yourself into the MOST POSSIBLE category of candidate (those applying in Round 1).

Let's use this opportunity to toss out our first strategy:

Snarky Strategy #1

> **Apply to Wharton in Round 1.**
> **Apply well before the deadline if you can.**

Since you'll be applying to multiple schools along with Wharton, and since one of those schools is highly likely to be Columbia, simply due to their similarities, then we'll cover a multi-school app strategy here too:

> **If you're applying to both Wharton and Columbia, as many people do, and you're more in love with Wharton than Columbia, then you should not do the Columbia Early Decision option.**

We very frequently see those who gain admission to one of these schools also have similar good luck with the other. This is because both schools look for similar traits, and to a slight degree, their applications require the same strategy. So if you're liking Wharton first and foremost, do their app in Round 1, and then submit to Columbia in their Regular Round.

To be clear, for most applicants, the advantage you'd get from a Columbia Early Decision app outweighs any advantage that a Wharton Round 1 app offers over Wharton Round 2. In other words, the same candidate might have better luck at Columbia ED than Wharton Round 1. If you like both these schools equally, then do Columbia Early Decision in order to increase your odds of getting in at one. But only do that if you will truly be satisfied with going to Columbia. Do not do Columbia Early Decision and Wharton Round 1 if you think you would choose Wharton over Columbia. An ED applicant to Columbia is giving their word that they will go there. Don't be the person who is so casual with commitments.

Obviously you need a strong application in any case. We're trying to lay out the different permutations for you to consider, since people often grapple with exactly these sorts of decisions.

If you like both Wharton and Harvard, then do both those apps in Round 1 – provided you're ready. There is an advantage to a Round 1 application at all of these top schools. Our commentary on Columbia Early Decision above is to try and explain that there's an *additional* advantage if you use that option – but you must be committed to Columbia wholeheartedly, because it's binding.

Enough about Columbia and Harvard and the rest. The point here? Apply to Wharton in the earliest round that you can, and yes, now the Wharton adcom is even inviting candidates to submit their applications before the respective round deadline.

What is "early"? About a month ahead of time should give you a leg up. Just make sure you're ready!! That's truly the most important thing – don't rush it in an attempt to be one of the early birds. A half-baked app submitted in August is not going to get you anywhere. As one admissions director says, "Don't hurry to get bad news." Take your time, and submit when you're ready.

Wharton's is not a true rolling process such as Columbia has – you won't get your final Wharton admit/deny decision earlier than their published decision dates – but you'll have more options for scheduling an interview earlier on, so they encourage apps to come in sooner rather than later.

Traits of a Wharton Admit

Before we dig into the essay(s), let's talk about the type of candidate who Wharton often responds well to – and before we do that, we wanted to share with you an honest article from a Class of 2014 in the Wharton student paper about the culture:

http://whartonjournal.com/2014/05/21/our-wharton-brand/

There are some telling moments in that piece that point to some attitudes that we have seen among people at not just Wharton but some other top business schools too. Wharton students used to have a reputation that was much worse than it is now, but it's still not the same perception you tend to get about students at, say, UC-Berkeley. This is another point of evidence to show you that culture matters, and that you should also do your own research into what the programs are like and how their communities feel to you personally.

Moving on. Who gets in to Wharton?

The elements of a successful profile for admission to The Wharton School tend to be:

> **1. Work Experience. Wharton** prefers more experienced, and thus somewhat older, candidates. They say that on average, students have between five and six years of work experience. If you're still in school or just graduated, this is probably not the best place to apply to unless you've got amazing evidence of how you've been a superstar all along. They also are going to have trouble admitting someone straight from a graduate program unless you had some time in the workforce in between.
>
> - *What's a "minimum" number of years of work experience?* We strongly recommend having at least three years of work experience before trying for Wharton.
>
>   That being said, about a quarter of their students are early in their careers – with 0-3 years under their belts – so it's not impossible to get even if you only graduated from college fairly recently. But you should know that a good chunk of those admitted with less work experience are *women*. We'll talk more about the female angle at Wharton in a bit. For now, just recognize that they have a lot more leniency on their work experience preferences for the ladies – not because they've got different standards for the sexes, but because they are very aware that women prefer to get bschool out of the way earlier in life, before they start to think about having kids. The Wharton adcom doesn't want to risk losing the high-potential female applicant simply because she has just two, instead of four, years in the workplace.

- **Is there a maximum age?** Not really. Most Wharton F/T MBA students are in their late 20s, with a number in their 30s, and there's someone in his 40s – or older! – in most classes. The only wrinkle if you're older (hahahaha pun intended) is that you'll be expected to know why an MBA is necessary at this stage and how you'll leverage it into a new position in the workforce, and the adcom will probably want to see ever-more impressive stories of achievement in your profile than they would a younger candidate, only because you've had more time to rack them up.

2. **Career, both past and future.** As we've been saying, Wharton is not "just" a finance school though certainly that's a strength. They also offer a lot of other very strong concentrations including real estate and entrepreneurship and more. They obviously send a lot of graduates to Wall Street and to the major consulting firms. Wharton is friendly to candidates from a variety of backgrounds and given how they're trying to expand their branding and enlarge the footprint, they may be especially welcoming to applicants from non-traditional industries or other functions besides the standard.

3. **GMAT** (or GRE). Wharton is agnostic about which test you present; either is fine. EssaySnark feels that there are still advantages to the GMAT over the GRE (we cover this on the blahg), but don't fret if all you have is the latter – provided it's a strong one. Just recognize that a very small number of people are accepted with a GRE score (only about 5%). We have no way of knowing if that's due to a small proportion of the applicant pool presenting the GRE, or if it shakes out in some other way. All of EssaySnark's discussions around tests focus on the GMAT because it's the standard.

In the past, Wharton has stated publicly that they prefer to see a balanced GMAT score of at least 80th percentile on both the quant and the verbal. We assume that those metrics hold for the GRE, too. Because of Wharton's large class size, they have the luxury of being able to admit students from a broader range of profiles without adversely affecting their averages too much.

However, an 80th percentile on the GMAT quant is harder and harder to achieve these days. Based on the current percentile breakdowns, if you ended up with a 48Q (78%), that's close enough. And they are flexible, in terms of looking at the entirety of your profile. The 80% percentile or higher thing is a preference, not a rule. You do not even need to be above the 700 mark on your GMAT to get into Wharton (particularly if you're a woman – *ouch* that sounds like a diss – we'll dive into this sensitive topic more in a moment).

Of course, a high GMAT helps – and we predict it will help even more this year, given all that we said about Wharton putting Harvard in its sights and focusing on the GMAT as a way to get there. The importance of a high GMAT is always more true for certain classes of applicants than for others.

If you're going into finance, or if you've been in finance, and you don't score well on the quant side of the GMAT, you may have a tougher time of it during the admissions process here or at any school, since obviously you're going to need those skills in your career. Even though Wharton had a student with a GMAT score in the 570 range in the past few years, it's really not common there. Your profile will need to be *superlative* in terms of diversity or differentiation for you to have a shot at Wharton with a <660 GMAT. And it needs to be very strong if your GMAT is <700.

Also, it's fine to apply with a GMAT test taken before June 2012, before they introduced the Integrated Reasoning component – having one, or not having one, will not make a difference to your application one way or the other. The important thing is that if the I/R was part of the test when you took it, then you must have completed that section; they require a score for every section that was active at the time.

4. **GPA.** Wharton has traditionally given less leeway to applicants who have rocky academics. Anything below a 3.0 GPA will be a challenge for you. If your GMAT and your GPA are both below the school's averages, you're going to have to work hard to compensate for these weaknesses, and our optimism for your chances starts to fade. Remember, they want to see Harvard-quality candidates, and those are the ones with stellarness across the entire kaleidoscope of their application. Nobody's profile is flawless, but those who get into these schools have way more strengths than faults.

We discuss both low GPA and low GMAT in many topics on the blahg at http://essaysnark.com

These are broad-strokes guidelines, not set-in-stone rules for what Wharton wants and how they'll react to a given profile. Everyone's got some weaknesses. Your job is to show the adcom how those weaknesses are not showstoppers, based on all your other great strengths.

The other common trait among accepted Wharton applicants that we need to comment on is not something you have much control over:

5. **Being female.** OK, at risk of being accused of sexism and all sorts of untoward things, we are still going to call it as we see it. Wharton doesn't *prefer* women, but they surely will give you a warm welcome if you happen to be one.

Just a few years back, Wharton's female enrollment numbers were highest of any school, ever, at 45%. The Class of 2014 dipped down to 42% and it stayed steady there for 2015. This is above Harvard's number of 41% for the classes of 2015 and 2016 (we had actually expected the Class of 2016 to move higher in terms of female students at HBS, given all the negative publicity that they experienced around gender and class issues in Fall of 2013). So this is at least one metric where presumably Wharton is maintaining equity or even besting Harvard. We don't have Wharton 2016 numbers available yet to say how it shook out last season, and time will tell if they're able to keep these figures high.

Why do we make the radical claim that Wharton will accept women with lower GMAT scores? Because of the results we witness – and because the entire population of women taking the GMAT shows that women simply do not fare as well on the test. Maybe it's the lingering "I can't do math" fallacy that girls often pick up in grade school and that is reinforced by certain cultures. Many women do great on the GMAT math but there are fewer women overall, and a smaller subset of those come in with the super high scores. If Wharton wants to admit more women, then they had to acknowledge that the GMAT scores will not be as high in all cases.

Also, at least a few years back, we saw Wharton accept some women who we felt were a little borderline in their qualifications. We were there each step of the way with these women as they applied. We know what their apps looked like. We know where they tried for and where they got in. These are women who did not make it at Harvard, Stanford, or Kellogg. But they got in at Wharton. OK great, more power to them! We're not faulting the women. But those outcomes are a little suspicious. Typically, someone who makes it into Wharton also gets offers at other schools. It's pretty rare that someone ends up with a Wharton admit and no other choices in hand. What was Wharton seeing that the other schools did not?

And, let's just break this down in the realm of logic: There's no way in h3ll that all these women accepted at Wharton had ONLY applied to Wharton. OK, maybe a handful of them did single-school app strategies, sure. But these are candidates who most likely applied to multiple programs – just like you are going to do. The coup that Wharton has pulled off is in getting so many of them women to *accept their offer* over other schools – and that is commendable. But we also strongly suspect that Wharton started accepting a number of women that other top-top schools took a pass on.

We do know that Wharton will accept a strong woman who's on the younger side, whereas with a man with a similar profile who's the same age, they may take a pass, just based on their preference for more work experience. Someone who's more seasoned is going to make a bigger contribution in the classroom and will be a greater asset to their peers (at least, that's the theory). Dean Robertson said in an interview a few years ago that accepting women with less work experience is the compromise they've decided to make, given the reality that the MBA is competing with many women's desire to have a family. *Get 'em while they're young* is a tactic being deployed at many bschools.

And the overall number of women applying to bschool may be going up – the GMAC is reporting that more women are taking the GMAT year over year. So it's natural that all schools will see their ratio of female students rise. But even so, the GMAC's last set of data indicates that only 40% of GMAT test-takers are women. Most people who take the GMAT do not score anywhere near a range that would be acceptable to a Top 10 school. The overall pool of qualified women candidates might be increasing, but it's questionable by how much.

So do the math, or use those analytical skills that Wharton says they value so much. Is it honestly possible that Wharton is maintaining the same standards of selectivity across the board for their female applicants? Sorry, but we strongly doubt it. They've boosted their enrollment of women by about 10% total the past few years. We just don't see where they got an additional 10% more qualified female applicants during those same periods – *especially when Wharton's application numbers went down for several years in a row.*

The takeaway? If you're a woman, and you like Wharton, you should DEFINITELY apply – you still need a strong GMAT score and hopefully you have a nice GPA to go with it, but if those scores aren't what you're proudest of, and/or you're on the young side, or if you're coming from a non-traditional background, you may not find those factors to be the obstacles here that they might be elsewhere.

Wharton has led the charge in boosting the proportion of women walking the halls, and other schools have since been scrambling to try and catch up. We're certain that one reason Wharton got such high numbers of women students is due to the dedicated outreach that they're doing for women candidates, work that they started several years back that is now bearing fruit. Once a woman is accepted to Wharton – even if she's also been accepted to Columbia and Harvard – she may choose Wharton simply because she knows that Wharton is putting the emphasis on women. That's probably a reassuring feeling for the candidate, and it's likely a big part of the reason that these percentages have moved higher at this school.

If you're a guy? Please don't be upset by this. It sounds like favoritism and it's easy to get self-righteous about the unfairness of it – but things have been unfair for women for a really long time. Private universities are allowed to make whatever admissions decisions they want. The U.S. Supreme Court recently affirmed the practice of affirmative action in admissions (sort of). It's a sticky subject and we can see both sides of the argument.

Anyway, there's all sorts of studies now that show that when women are in leadership positions, on the executive teams, and on the board of directors, companies tend to be more profitable. This intentional adjustment is probably a good thing for all of us – and it's also in the category of something you have no control over. Don't get your boxers in a twist over it. (If you're a single guy, then the dating scene may be tough... but there's all those undergrads at Wharton too, so, silver lining?)

The takeaway message *for everyone* is that you need to focus all your energies into putting together the strongest pitch that you can for your own personal profile and set of circumstances. Write a killer set of essays. Pick the strongest set of recommenders possible. Put your ducks in a row and submit early, with the knowledge that you put in your best shot.

And since that's what EssaySnark is all about, then maybe it is time to finally get started on that.

Your Wharton Application Strategy

Here are the fundamentals you need to know as you start to craft your Wharton essay strategy.

What to do when

We already said you should apply to Wharton in the *earliest round possible*, and you should apply *early in the round*.

Now that you know you have to get busy, then what order should you tackle the actual application components in? Essays and recommendations and resume – oh my! What do you do first? Obviously this is not what the Wharton admissions peeps had in mind when they stated that "timing" is important, but you, as the developer of a sound strategy, should be looking at all the pieces holistically.

Here's one approach:

Snarky Strategy #2

Write your essay(s). Figure out your theme.

Then hit up your recommenders to do their thing.

Why this order? Why not start by getting your recommenders on board first? After all, that part is easy. You could totally get them started, and feel like you're making progress on your application, when really all you're doing is procrastinating on writing the darn essays.

What EssaySnark suggests is, **get through at least the first couple drafts of your essay(s) before talking to your boss about writing her rec.** The reason for this? *Then you'll know where the holes are in your profile, and you can suggest ideas for what your boss can write about in their first recommender's question that can fill those holes.* Remember, the adcom is going to look at your application as a whole. All the pieces should work together. Not only is it important that every element of your app reinforce the others, but it's also a critical strategic opportunity for you.

This is an often overlooked strategy that can really help the school see the big picture, and it can give you a little more control over how you're presenting. (Note, too, that such "what should I write about" conversations with your recommenders are perfectly fine, as long as you don't actually write their recommendations yourself!!)

If you want a whole tutorial on who to choose as your recommenders and how to prep them, check out the EssaySnark App Accelerator on Letters of Recommendation – it's advertised on our website at essaysnark.com. All App Accelerators include feedback from EssaySnark, so this one on your recommenders lets you submit your plans for your recommendations strategy to us and we'll let you know if it's sound or not optimal.

Back to Wharton. The takeaway message here is write the essay FIRST. Then go talk to your recommenders about what they might be able to say about you – with some clear suggestions on how their messaging can add the most value to your pitch.

Anyway, letters of recommendation will be simpler this year than ever before. Because of how many schools including Wharton have collaborated to standardize their recommendation questions, down to two pretty easy ones, the burden on your recommenders should be lessened significantly. No need to rush into that piece of the puzzle until you're ready for it. Take your time to get your own ducks in a row, and then go to your recommenders with a strategy for how each of them can best maximize the limited space that they will have in writing about new examples to add breadth and depth to your application for the adcom.

The 5 key points of a Wharton "gain" essay

We often call the MBA application a "pitch" and it very much should be considered a marketing vehicle. Not "marketing" as in false promises and lots of hype, but "marketing" as in proper positioning and offering a solid product to your audience – one they can believe in, that they will want to "buy" (or, *accept*). You are marketing YOU.

Your essays are your best opportunity to do that, though the pitch is much more than just the essays. You'll present yourself again, in an even more direct way, when you get the chance to do the interview (or team-based discussion, whatever). You should also recognize though that the objective for each of those steps is totally different.

Just like in a big-ticket or enterprise sales process, at the first point of contact, you're not trying to get the customer to buy; you're trying to get them to move to the next phase of the process. To use that analogy here, your application – specifically, the essay – is not supposed to get you admitted. It's supposed to meet the needs that the adcom has in deciding to *invite you to interview*. Then, there's a different objective with the interview (mostly it's not to screw things up!) but that is another conversation entirely.

For now, the bulk of your attention needs to be focused directly on creating a pitch that gets you in the door – that gets you the interview.

Here are the key criteria your main Wharton essay should meet:

1. It must communicate what you want to do in your future career, immediately post-bschool – *specifically*

2. It must show why you need an MBA to go do that – *preferably why you need a Wharton MBA*

3. It must demonstrate that you're ready for this big challenge – *with examples*

4. It should express your appreciation for the Wharton advantage – *this is how you show "school fit"*

5. Ideally it will also give some insights into how you're differentiated, who you are, what you're about – *this needs to happen in the main essay, not the optional ones*

You may want to come back to this 5-point list after you've written your draft, to see how it stacks up. Keep the focus first and foremost on professional highlights or achievements, and a future-leaning statement of career goals and why you want an MBA.

And don't forget to include a direct answer to the "what will you gain?" question.

What do they mean by "substance"?

Remember when we called out the "timing, presentation, and substance" thing from the Wharton website? The "substance" part is absolutely critical. The adcom won't be able to get a sense of who you are as a person if you talk at a high level, in vague terms, in the essays. You need to be thorough.

The *substance* of your application means you are giving the reader something to go on – you're using examples to illustrate your key points, you're offering details about what you want to do, you're giving precise answers to the questions. Doing so will create a meaty app, and meaty apps are fun to chew on.

(Sorry if that grossed out the vegans in the room.)

Where do you need to show details?

On the career goals.

And on how you're qualified.

Oh yeah: Don't forget to include a direct answer to the part about "what will you gain?"

Career Goals

A very important aspect of the Wharton admissions process is your career goals. This is the core of your pitch, the immediate rationale behind why you are applying in the first place. The career goals should be driving your strategy.

One reason that people who are admitted to Columbia often see a similar outcome at Wharton is because both schools care a lot about the goals. Columbia probably cares a little more about them, but both examine them closely. If you're applying to both schools, you may want to do the Columbia career goals essay first (and hammer out their short-answer question too obviously) – and then circle back to Wharton.

A 500-word essay to Wharton should be totally sufficient to do a good job on the goals (one year the Wharton career goals essay was just 300 words – ouch). This year, they have also maintained an important angle in their career goals question: the bit about "through the Wharton MBA." Several years ago, they just asked candidates to describe the goals without including an element of "why Wharton" in the question at all.

The easiest way to answer this?

Just tell the adcom why you want to go there.

Why do you want an MBA?

Yeah, we know. Sorta obvious. Yet you would be SHOCKED – yes, SHOCKED – at how many people fail to answer that very simple question with anything valuable at all.

Do you know why you want an MBA?

Now would be a very good time to start thinking about it.

Sometimes people get caught up in the glamor of it. It sounds exciting. Prestigious. All my friends have one.

What is the actual purpose of it, though?

Please take some time to jot down your responses for this. They should be very individual and unique to you; nobody else can provide justification for this.

After all, it's expensive. You'll be uprooting your life for two years to go live in a new place. Why bother?

What do you expect to gain from the experience?

This will likely require some soul-searching, and it may also help especially to talk to a wide range of people who have MBAs, from Wharton and other schools, to get their perspectives – not so that you can crib the things they say into your essays, but to see what the value is coming out, and how people talk about their experiences. See what resonates from you.

Reflect on it, and layer back in your goals – personal and professional (though the emphasis needs to be on career here).

With Wharton, this is not a complicated question, but your response may be quite complex. Or maybe a better word is multi-dimensional. Or nuanced. Or layered.

There is surely not one answer to this.

But remember that the answer you give is for one specific school.

Sure, you'll be able to pursue the same or similar goals at other schools too, but what makes Wharton unique in terms of the opportunities you'll have?

These are all things to think about.

Take copious notes.

Do brainstorming on these aspects.

Then when you're ready to write: Start with the goals, explain why Wharton is a good fit for you, then explain why you're a good fit for Wharton. Tell them about why you want an MBA, and why you need to get it here.

How do you do it?

Start with your goals.

Wharton wants to know what you want to do after you graduate with your MBA, and they want to know the SPECIFICS. EssaySnark has for years asked all of our clients to do what we call a "Career Goal Statement" as the very first step of our consulting engagement. You would benefit from going through this process, too.

EssaySnark's career goals exercise for new clients

Please complete this fill-in-the-blank exercise. This is a good first step for you to develop your ideas for career goals, in order to demonstrate to the adcom what you want to do and why an MBA is essential:

1. "After I get my MBA I will be/do X" [add as much detail as you can - job title, industry or niche, functional area, specialty, example companies to work for, geography, etc.].

[Write your answer here. Go ahead. Nobody will look at it.]

_____

_____

_____

_____

2. "My long term goal is to do Y" [less detail needed but must be clear and specific, and rational, given the s/t goal]

[Write this one down, too.]

_____

_____

_____

_____

> **3. "An MBA from Wharton is critical for me to achieve this because: "** [solid reasons that point to the differentiation offered by Wharton are critical here — you'll want to express how it will explicitly give you the skills you need for the short-term goal]
>
> *[This bit is important. Use more space if you need to.]*
>
> _____
>
> _____
>
> _____

Yes, even though Wharton isn't asking for a "title" – nor are they even asking for short-term versus long-term goals – it wouldn't hurt to tackle this as if they have, at least for your purposes in planning it out. These details can demonstrate to the adcom that you've done your homework and have a true plan for the future. Whether you actually use terminology like "short-term goal" is up to you – they've asked for "professional objectives" so you have some leeway in terms of how you actually express these things. Just remember that specificity can take you far. It shows that you've put some thought into it, that you've researched the options, that you know the industry. That level of detail truly cannot hurt you.

The school experience needs to be the setup for the short-term goal; bschool should be positioned as the best means possible to prepare you for that. The long-term goal needs less detail, but it needs to be logical and achievable, given the interim goals. You wouldn't want to position bschool as prep for the l/t goal, only the short-term one.

You might not need to explicitly state your goals in these terms in the main Wharton essay since it's not how they've asked the question – but you should know the answers to these elements, for sure.

The EssaySnark Career Goals App Accelerator walks you through several structured exercises to identify the components of your career goals. We've found that process to be immensely helpful for Brave Supplicants applying to career-goals-intensive schools like Wharton (and Columbia, and NYU, and Booth, and Duke, and Haas, and many many others).

So what's a bad career goal?

Let's look at some examples of career goals that are too vague and ill-defined.

> "I want to become a leader in the financial services industry."

We see this all the time. Sorry folks. "Leader" is meaningless. And, believe it or not, so is "financial services." Much too broad. Are you talking about a big bank? A hedge fund? A mutual fund or other investment management company? Even insurance companies are often lumped into "financial services." This sentence is near-meaningless. It doesn't tell us anything about *what you want to do*.

Here's another one:

> "I want to be on the executive team of a multinational corporation."

Same problem. Sure, "executive team" has a little more specificity than "leader" however it still doesn't tell us *what you want to do*. (Note the theme?) And "multinational corporation" is just a blob of a term. What type of corporation? In which country? If you're interested in some type of international angle to your career, then you need to say that! This term is communicating next to nothing — except to say that maybe you haven't really put that much thought into it yet.

The other issue with both of these (probably) is timing. It's unrealistic to assume you'll be much of a "leader" — at least, not on a grand scale or anything — within the timeframe that Wharton is asking you to present with these career goals. Nobody can see the future. Nobody knows what you'll be doing in 15 years. And that's how long it takes for most people to gain the experience, skills, and connections to actually become a CFO or what have you. It's highly unlikely you'll be rocking that boat within the timeframe expected in a "short/long-term goals" question from any school.

Instead, you need to focus on literally what type of job you'll get right when you come out of Wharton, and then possibly extend that out to what you see yourself doing in the distance. The way you pitch your goals to Wharton doesn't have to be quite as structured and buttoned-up as you'd do for Columbia, but surely it wouldn't hurt.

Here's even a little bit of space for you to capture your thinking on this. Yes, right here. Go ahead.

One exception where it might fly to tell the adcom that you'll be "CEO"? If you're going to be working in a family business after you graduate. If that's the case, then it's fine to say you're going to be taking over the whole show. You have different challenges than most people in presenting your goals (which are outside the discussion of this guide) however this could work fine in being realistic and believable.

But we've gotten ahead of ourselves. All this goes in the first essay. We were still looking at just that short-answer question. Let's go back. Let's talk about that "realistic and believable" thing.

It's so important that we're making it

Snarky Strategy #3

Your career goals must be both realistic and *believable.*

The Wharton adcom is really, truly, going to look at your goals and see if they make sense. Is this a plan that you will be able to pull off? Is it do-able? Or more like a pipe dream?

The important takeaway message here is: *don't make stuff up.* The point of this exercise is not to present the most amazing, aggressive, flamboyant-sounding goals the school has ever seen. Actually, it's usually much more effective to present goals that are very standard, traditional, perhaps even run-of-the-mill.

Bschool candidates are always told that they have to stand out, that they have to differentiate themselves. Well guess what? The career goals is not the place to do this.

- **People are admitted to Wharton because they have clear, rational, logical goals that Wharton knows they can help them achieve.**

- **People are admitted to Wharton because the Wharton MBA is obviously going to be an accelerator for them to achieve success in their lives, to go out and contribute to the world (and, hopefully, to contribute to Wharton as an alumni later on).**

The best way to impress the Wharton adcom is to show them that you've already worked hard and built your education/career up to a certain point, and that you have a plan for where you want to take it from here, and you're looking for the advantage of a Wharton MBA to do so.

This means, you want to present career goals that MAKE SENSE, both given who YOU are, and given what WHARTON is.

This is the essence of "school fit" (a term that gets bandied about in bschool admissions circles and which many people have no clue about).

- If you're looking to use bschool to make some **radical career change**, you have a bigger challenge. You need to show the adcom that you have transferable skills and are equipped to make the transition to the new field. This can be especially critical for those going in a dissimilar direction, e.g., IT guys wanting to go into finance. You'll need to show how you're ready to make this leap.

- Conversely, if you're not showing ENOUGH transition — if your stated **short-term goal is too similar** (or even identical) to what you are already currently doing in your job today — then you're not giving the adcom enough evidence of why you need an MBA. You should position yourself as ADVANCING, and then show how the MBA is the one main requirement that you need to get from A to B.

A Snarky Caveat

The three most common mistakes with many career goals are:

* They're too vague

* They're too ambitious

* They're too broad

If your goals suffer from any of these sins, it's highly unlikely Wharton will let you in. Too vague means terminology like "financial services" or "executive team." Too ambitious is a goal that's written to impress the reader instead of being attainable for the candidate's actual skills and experience. Too broad is often when the applicant can't make up his mind and so he brings in multiple options of "I could do this or I might do that." While it could very well be true that you will pursue different options and paths once you're in the process of earning your MBA, it is usually a mistake to try and present all these different options to the Wharton adcom in their essays. There simply isn't room to provide an appropriate level of detail on more than one possible career path.

The Wharton adcom tends to reward candidates who express confidence and conviction, who sound like they have an honest-to-goodness action plan. Sure, your life may take you in a different direction once the wheels are in motion. What the Wharton folks want to see is that you're mature and responsible, that you know how to take control of your life and that you're able to make your own success. A well-crafted set of Wharton essays will communicate this implicitly (no, we do not recommend that you literally tell the adcom that you have done that or are that type of person).

In a nutshell: Keeping that *realistic and believable* guideline in mind as you refine your goals should help you avoid these problems.

The Wharton Essay:
What You Will Gain (aka Professional Objectives)

Wharton asks:

> What do you ~~aspire~~ hope to gain, personally and professionally, through the Wharton MBA? (500 words)

At some point between the time they originally released the essay questions in June (when the first version of this 2014 guide was published) and Round 1, Wharton changed the verb "aspire" to "hope". Interesting. Simpler language is always a benefit to everyone.

This version is also different from last year's question:

- They used to ask *"What do you want to achieve?"*
- Now it's *"What do you want to gain?"*

This is actually a slightly puzzling change, from our perspective. "Achieve" to us is an action verb, that's focusing on what you will do, the effort you will put in.

"Gain" just sounds like something will be handed to you... and that's totally not how any part of the MBA experience works.

But there's much more to it, as we referenced in our earlier suggestion to go talk to people who have MBAs. Business school is often talked about as a "transformative experience."

- What changes do you want to see in yourself, your life, and your overall capacities as a human being as a result of your time at Wharton?
- Where do you want to be in life?
- What kind of person do you think Wharton can help shape you into?
- What experiences at Wharton do you predict are going to be the most beneficial in helping you get there?

Any or potentially all of these angles – or many others instead – could possibly be explored in your essay.

Just don't forget to *answer the question*. And focus on the actual goals will help you tremendously.

What needs to go in this main essay?

Or, *how to do it.*

First, this essay needs to FOCUS ON THE FUTURE. You'll notice they ask nothing about the past. They can read your resume to know your professional history.

That being said, it's definitely relevant to include a quick recap of who you are/what you've done, to set context. This can be really helpful to the reader and it is where you will satisfy point #3 on that list of tips we offered earlier (page 23). Just **do not go overboard**. There probably needs to be only a couple sentences of background info at the very most, or a very short paragraph. You need to be sharing your appreciation for how you, with that unique background that you've referenced, will be in the best position possible to make the most of the Wharton experience.

As an example, a straightforward structure for the Wharton essay might be (yours need not conform exactly):

- **INTRO: We always prefer to see a direct answer to the question right upfront.** It can even be as obvious as "At Wharton, I aspire to gain..." although that's a little clumsy. Or you can get more creative with something like: "Based on my three years in private equity, I am now ready to go to business school so that I can pursue the next challenge of moving into venture capital." (And it goes without saying that if we ever see that sentence in an essay, we will throttle you – this is just an example to illustrate a point. You need to *write your own essays*. Besides the fact that that sentence is actually quite generic and doesn't really share much about you at all; it could be much much richer.)

- Any foundation info on your career to date would also work well in the intro – just make sure it's concrete. As we just mentioned in that sketch sentence above, it didn't communicate hardly anything. Instead, tell a quick story or give an example if possible. To illustrate: "Since joining ABC Partners as an Analyst in 2008, I have built strong skills in this and that through my success leading such-and-such projects." Notice that we have actual details (or placeholders for details) here: we've told the reader the company name, our current job title, how long we've been on the job, and we've fed in some statements of achievement and started to express our competencies. You'd want this foundational info to give the reader a little context without going overboard. Or, you could cover this later on — or possibly not at all, depending on your approach to this essay — however it often flows nicely to start from the past and use a linear structure that flows along a timeline of what you intend to do when.

- **PARA 2 (1/3 of essay): Professional objectives, aka short-term goal.** You need to give the details to give it life. Define/explain/express/illustrate what you want to do when you graduate from Wharton. This should probably be a full paragraph

- **PARA 3: Long-term goal – this is technically optional**, given how they've phrased the question, though it's recommended to have at least a directional target for where you want to go later. This can be a quick sentence, or maybe a full paragraph but a shorter one. You need much less detail here.

- **PARA 4 (1/3 of essay):** Why MBA/why Wharton? The focus should be on the latter, which implicitly answers the former.

- **CONCLUSION**: Wrap up with a recap of why you want an MBA from Wharton, ideally restating your career goals and/or referencing something specific about the program, etc. Can be just a sentence or two but please don't skip the conclusion.

Notice that we didn't actually say anything in that structure above about what you want to gain "personally." This might be something to explore but it is NOT MANDATORY. We saw plenty of good essays that stuck only to the professional side for this question last year. Maybe you could talk about some of the extracurricular experiences at Wharton in answer to this part – but with only 500 words to work with, it is often an area that needs to get sacrificed. Many people who will try to manufacture some answer to the "personal gains" part of this question will flounder. Don't force it. If our prior questions about how you envision your life changing post-Wharton triggered some ideas for you, then great, include those, but don't feel like you're missing something important if you choose not to.

Snarky Strategy #4

The focus of your essay should be *professional aspirations*.

You're going to bschool to advance your career. Those career goals form the foundation of your Wharton application. Everything else you present should in some way reinforce these goals. You risk muddying the waters or talking in vague platitudes if you try to include too much stuff about "personal" achievements.

Obviously some people may have a "personal" angle to their interest in Wharton. Maybe your mother went there, or your family is from Pennsylvania. These are tertiary reasons but they count.

Back to the personal angles with this essay. If you are passionate and highly involved in a specific charity or worthwhile cause that's outside your career, certainly it would warrant a discussion if relevant to your planned Wharton experience.

However beyond that, it's hard for us to imagine too many personal achievements that anyone is going to make at bschool. There can certainly be exceptions to this – Wharton does offer some interesting opportunities that we know of which are outside the classroom and beyond the definition of the straight-up professional achievement of advancing your career. However we are not going to suggest those to you. You're invited to research the school and uncover them on your own. If we spoonfed those to you here then everyone would include the same ones in their Wharton essay and that would suck.

What we can offer are the buzzwords that Wharton was touting at the time of the launch of their new curriculum a few years ago:

Social Impact, Global Presence, and Innovation

If your career goals dovetail with any of these ideas, then they would be good to explore in the essay.

In addition, you can spend some time reflecting on what type of "personal gains" you might expect from the bschool experience. If you come up with something good, then you should most certainly include it in your Wharton essay.

But we don't think it's technically necessary.

And yes, that's a first. Last year's version of this question was the first time that we had ever suggested that applicants willfully disregard part of a school's essay question. There may be some who disagree with this advice. You need to call this using your own evaluation and judgment.

Wharton and You

Two bits of advice to mention here:

First: If you attended Wharton (or Penn) as an undergrad, then that's worth mentioning – just note that you may be expected to do MORE with your Wharton essay based on your status as an alum than the adcom would look for from another candidate.

We have often had Brave Supplicants who were Wharton alums come to us after being rejected, wondering what went wrong. Frequently, these candidates don't do nearly enough to convince the adcom why they're choosing Wharton again; they seem to assume that going there once is evidence enough that they would want to go there again. This is where the "pitch" comes in and the bar is set a bit higher for alumni of the school.

Second: Make sure that everything you include in this essay adds up to a logical and complete picture.

What we mean by that is, everything needs to be internally consistent.

If your first paragraph is all about how you want to go into private equity – about a quarter of incoming students say that's what they want to do – then we'd be a little puzzled if, in the very next paragraph, you start talking about Wharton's social venture initiatives and a mentoring program that they have. Maybe those opportunities could fit in at the very end, but you first need to give some backup to your goals.

The school has put an emphasis on ACADEMICS. We can see that in their GMAT and GPA numbers. They even had an entire essay question about it last year:

from 2013:

> Academic engagement is an important element of the Wharton MBA experience. How do you see yourself contributing to our learning community?

Just because they ditched that question from the line-up doesn't mean that academics are not a key part of the MBA experience. ("Like, duh, EssaySnark.") Their extracurricular opportunities totally fall under the umbrella of this essay too – but off to the side. When you talk about Wharton, please don't neglect to talk about how you will engage in some academic activities that will allow you to become a winner in your stated future career.

A common mistake: Not sharing enough of yourself

Since this question doesn't ask you to talk about your background or your personal interests or your unique experiences or any other noun that points you to something in your past and history, then isn't it OK to make the whole thing about what you want to do at Wharton?

No.

We said already that this should be future-focused and what we mean by that is, you should be talking in active terms about how you will be pursuing the goals you've set for yourself through the opportunities available at The Wharton School.

But the best way to show that you are CURRENTLY in a position to actually TAKE ADVANTAGE of those opportunities is to layer in some examples of what you've done to date that qualifies you to pursue them.

So please, remember that a chunk of this essay's content should be actually talking about yourself.

What specifically should you share about yourself with this question?

Maybe one or two soundbite examples of how you've been an overachiever, or done something distinctive, or in some way had an accomplishment or success in your life that puts you ahead of your peers and shows you as someone who will hit the ground running and take the bull by its horns and many other testosterone-filled analogies (that are appropriate for women too, after all women have drive and ambition just as much as men do).

This example you present doesn't have to be from the workforce – though it could be. You could talk about something personal to you, a situation or circumstance that made you who you are. That's completely fair game for this essay, provided you are able to appropriately connect it in to the rest of the answer that you give to the question that they have asked.

It might be appropriate to talk about something really personal, like how you grew up in a poor family, but again you'll need to do so with a deft hand, and connect it back to your answer of what you will gain from Wharton. Don't toss out random factoids into the essay unless they really do support the answer you're offering. Everything must add up, as we said before.

You may find it easier to stick with the purely professional realm. There are some obvious choices — for an obvious example, someone who wants to start her own business might talk about participating in a Wharton business plan competition, as a way to reinforce her business idea. *But she also needs to talk about how she is ready to pursue an entrepreneurial goal.* This is done through using an example from her past when she has done something entrepreneurial. (There are many many ways to demonstrate this, by the way, and it is critically important that you are able to do so if you're pitching entrepreneurship as your post-MBA goal.)

You will notice that this question is not simply asking you to present the courses and classes and clubs that you want to take. It's not meant for you to give a laundry list of Wharton stuff that you found on their website. While you may want to do some of that, to show how the school is a good fit for you, the focus needs to show how *you are a good fit for them.* You do this by getting specific, and detailed. You have a huge opportunity to reveal who you are based on the information you share with the adcom in this essay.

If our hypothetical candidate does decide to talk about the bplan comp, she should go into some details – go beyond the surface, give more than a pat, obvious answer. She needs to do more than just mention it. She needs to talk about it in the context of the question being asked. Take it to its full extent. If you want to participate in that competition, *then what? What will you gain from that?* Don't go on and on – and don't answer only the obvious, surface level stuff. Don't say, "I might win some money to fund my startup – uh, that doesn't work, both because there's no guarantee you'd win, and to say so is being perhaps a little overconfident, but also because that's sort of the point of entering a competition like that. Go beyond the obvious. Don't waste time telling the reader stuff that she already knows (and don't insult her intelligence).

Look for possible topics that can add texture and variety to your profile. Help the adcom know more about you by what you choose to present in this essay. You may want to do some brainstorming on this. Make a list of the most important projects that you've worked on. Identify your biggest wins, both personally and professionally. Reflect on what you learned and what you know from those experiences. Those insights about who you are and what you have can be great additions to this essay.

You can offer interesting insights into who you are in lots and lots of ways. Look for opportunities to do that through not only the Wharton-specific classes and resources that you mention, but in describing why you are mentioning them, and what you bring to the table. This is how you make a multidimensional essay that communicates to the adcom – and one that is memorable. This is how your essay will stand out from the crowd.

A very important suggestion

This year's single Wharton essay question unfortunately will cause many people to sound like "takers" when they write their essays.

"Takers" is a term that Wharton professor Adam Grant uses in his awesome book *Give and Take*. It's the type of person who goes through life with a gimme attitude.

If all you end up doing in your Wharton essay is talk about "what you will gain" – which is literally what they've asked you to talk about – then maybe you'll make it through the evaluation and into the interview. You won't have points marked against you for following the instructions to the letter. You will be following instructions, and what you do could very well be sufficient to get you to the next stage.

However, if you're able to expand your view of "gain" to also include the things that you might be able to share with others, well... you have the potential for a real winner of an essay.

(And by the way, if you're able to go through life with that perspective, then you're going to have a real winner of an incarnation on this planet, too.)

First and foremost we would expect you – uh, what did we say about this before – oh yeah, *answer the question.* And the question asks about what you will gain.

Once you get that out of the way, then boy oh boy it would be nice to see you also talk about how you would be able to make a contribution to your classmates inside the classroom or on team projects *based on the knowledge, experiences, and insights that you will carry with you to campus.*

In other words: Tell us why you're differentiated, and ready for bschool, and capable and qualified, through a quick story or example from your life that demonstrates the value you'll bring to your peers.

Nope, not easy, and yes, hard to fit in, but very doable if you put your mind to it.

This question is forcing applicants to *engage with the school before they apply*. This is really what all schools want their applicants to do, to make sure you understand what the MBA from that school is about. (Hint: Even if one of your other schools doesn't have an explicit question like this, be sure to do that research – you should include such references somewhere in essays if possible, or at a minimum, be prepared with this information when you go to interview!)

It is unfortunate that so many Brave Supplicants slap together an application to the school without bothering to really understand it. This essay question is the adcom's attempt to force candidates to research their programs.

What to include in your "Why Wharton" content

Based on the phrasing of the question, then it should go without saying that you need to cover "why Wharton" explicitly somewhere.

When you do, you'll want to:

1. Be specific – choose an actual class or club or whatever – don't talk in broad strokes about some vague feature of the Wharton experience.

2. Be selective – limit yourself to just a couple resources at the school. Why? 'Cuz you won't have space to go into sufficient detail on more than that, and because the focus needs to be on YOU most of all.

3. Be personal – link your answer back to something within your profile.

Your objective in writing this material is to implicitly – and possibly explicitly – tell the adcom: Why have you chosen Wharton, over the gazillion other great schools out there, to achieve these stated goals?

You would want to also tell them that you visited campus on [date] and got all inspired by [such and such]. Show them how much homework you've done on what they have ("homework" is not just reading the website, FYI). But, make it relevant. Link in these school-specific references to who you are, and where you're going.

You may want to do a formal gap analysis — see where you're lacking and how the Wharton education can fill those gaps, then identify the resources that will do it. This can be hard skills, soft skills, or both. Cite the ways you'll fill those gaps. Make all this tailored to Wharton.

You must work hard to a) do enough research into the Wharton offering that you can come up with something compelling to write about; and b) make it personal. Tie it back to *you*. The adcom knows all about the resources that their school offers.

Don't waste space explaining what a school trek is; they know what it is. Use the space available to explain why YOU chose that, how YOU would leverage it – why it would make a difference for YOUR goals.

Use the invitation of this essay to really explore Wharton. Put some time into thinking about how you'd use your experience there Show them how you'll become a valuable member of the school community.

The net result of this effort is that you'll be a much more educated consumer of what the school can offer to you — and, hopefully, you'll be a much better informed applicant who can show reasons why Wharton is the right place for you to get your MBA.

Shameless plug: The **Essay Ideas App Accelerator** can be invaluable – it offers a way for you to get feedback on your outlines – – your foundation – the entirety of your proposed essay strategy – *before* you write your drafts. Read more about it on the EssaySnark website at <u>essaysnark.com</u>.

So, to restate our 5-point list from page 24: Your Wharton essay should communicate:

- clear career goals
- who you are as a person
- how you'll use the Wharton experience

If you follow the suggested structure of the essay that we provided, and the 5-point list of what to put in it, you should have these things covered, no sweat.

Now the million-dollar questions:

Can I re-use my Wharton essay for Harvard?

No.

Can I re-use my Harvard essay for Wharton?

No.

However: If you come up with something compelling and important that you're sharing with Harvard then *maybe* – with a firm emphasis on the *maybe* – it could be appropriate to pare that back and submit in the main optional essay. We are skeptical that most people will pull this off appropriately for Wharton, but yes, there's a possibility that it could work. It truly depends on what you're saying and how you're saying it.

Can I re-use my Wharton essay for Stanford?

Stanford question 2 is similar, isn't it? Yes... and no. A similar strategy for Wharton may work for Stanford but you basically need to rewrite the whole thing from scratch if you think you'll have any hope at all in attracting the attention of the GSB. So again, the answer is "no" on this one too.

Can I re-use my Wharton essay for Columbia?

Maybe. Or at least, sort of. Of any of the schools that you might be able to repurpose some of your thinking for, Columbia and Wharton are actually closest.

Explanations

Wharton ↔ Harvard

The reason you should really not even be tempted to use the Wharton essay for Harvard or vice versa is because *Wharton does not really do their admissions evaluations the same as Harvard does.*

Plus, the questions are very different.

Like, VERY different.

If you try to use your structured Wharton essay for Harvard and just swap out names of classes and the like, then you will totally be missing the point of the Harvard question. Plus, the HBS Admissions Board will be able to spot that from a mile away. You should pick up the Harvard essay guide if you're not clear on the distinction and why this would be a mistake.

If you feel like you wrote a winner of an essay for Harvard and you're looking for ways to re-use that for Wharton, well, we haven't seen your Harvard essay so we can't say for sure, but our deep suspicion would be that one or the other ideas is woefully misguided.

Wharton ↔ Stanford

We're nervous about people trying to re-use these two essays, even though yes, your approach actually could be somewhat comparable, in terms of how you do the research and the types of things that you want to investigate about Stanford to pull into their essay 2. The essence of both Wharton's and Stanford's questions is, why do you want to come HERE for your MBA? Many of the strategies do overlap in terms of how you break down that question, and what you use in support of your answer after analyzing your own background and material. But what you actually end up saying is going to be so completely different for each school that you may as well write each one separately, from scratch. Sorry.

Wharton ↔ Columbia

However, there's hope! For all you time-starved and writing-exhausted Brave Supplicants trying for Wharton and Columbia, there is more opportunity here than with other schools.

As we mentioned earlier in this guide, those two schools are most alike in terms of how they evaluate applications. Wharton is now putting a much greater emphasis on GMAT and GPA, but in terms of what they look for and how they respond to essay content in particular, these two schools are really quite similar.

If you do a good job pitching one in its career goals essay, you're likely to have success with the other.

Now, the big risk with our saying you might be able to reuse parts of Wharton for Columbia (or vice versa) is that you'll end up totally botching it on the second school. The questions really are phrased very differently, and the answer you provide and how you structure your essay likely will need to be modified quite substantially from one school to the next.

It's the *thinking* and *ideas* and possibly the *reasons why you want an MBA* that can be re-used.

And of course the career goals.

There's no reason in the whole wide world that we can think of why you would be changing career goals from school to school. So the work you do on mapping out and clarifying and refining the goals in how you express them for Wharton could be totally reusable in the Columbia essay.

And the way you talk about how you're prepared to pursue those goals also could be pulled in to your next draft.

Just be so super careful and meticulous on how you proofread. You would not believe how many times the schools get essays with a different school's name in them. Talk about a turn-off to the adcom.

The schools know that your goals may change

This is a common question and we'll make the point right here: It's totally understandable that as you go through the process of pursuing your MBA, you may decide on a different course of action than your best thinking at the time.

However, in order to *get in* to a school like Wharton so that you can pursue that MBA, you need to articulate what "your best thinking at the time" is. You need to be thoughtful about how you articulate your current plans for the future. It's fine if you get called into a different direction of inspiration later on. The schools are looking for evidence that you can come up with a plan, that you're reasonable about your expectations and know what your own strengths are that you can build on, and that you understand why you want the MBA at all. That's it. If you can do that, you'll be far ahead of the pack.

The Optional Essays

These two essays really and truly are optional – but one is more "optional" than the other. PLEASE oh please oh please do not feel compelled to use either of these essays just because they're there, and just because Wharton has only the one required essay to work with.

The second optional essay, labeled "Optional Essay" in the online application, which talks about first-time applicants and reapplicants, should be used ONLY TO PROVIDE NEEDED INFORMATION THAT YOU CANNOT PRESENT ELSEWHERE, about specific gaps or weaknesses or holes in your profile. This one we call the *mandatory-if-your-situation-requires-it* optional essay (or, "mandatory-optional"). This is just like any other school's optional essay, where you can discuss:

- gaps in employment
- no recommendation from your current direct supervisor
- low GPA
- *maybe* low GMAT

We have lots of posts on the EssaySnark blahg about these issues and when it's appropriate to use them in the optional essay. There's a pretty small list of topics that qualify here. On this optional essay, our advice is true for any school, not just Wharton: If you don't have something specific that is a) important; and b) that you cannot cover appropriately in the main essay... then you should not write the mandatory-optional essay. However, if you do have one of these issues in your profile, then you MUST write the mandatory-optional essay.

Or to rephrase: Only write the mandatory-optional essay if you have a PROBLEM in your profile that you need to explain. The adcom gives clear examples of what would qualify. If you are a reapplicant, then this mandatory-optional essay needs to be used to talk about how you've improved your profile since last year.

Keep in mind that, as we've been saying over and over, Wharton puts an emphasis on grades, and so if you're going to call attention to a low GPA, then you'd better have some good reasons to offer AND you hopefully also can tell them about some class you've taken recently where you pulled an A and impressed the professor.

We cover the perennial question of "what to do about a low GPA" on our blahg (choose "GPA: from the dropdown category menu at the top right of the first page).

Another necessary use of the mandatory-optional essay is if you are not getting a letter of recommendation from your current supervisor. You should simply explain the situation (briefly!) in the optional essay, and tell the adcom why you chose the recommenders that you did instead of your supervisor. Ideally in such a case, at least one of your recommenders will be a supervisor from a previous job. Keep in mind that this optional essay should be SHORT. If all you're doing is explaining your choice of recommender, there's no reason why it should go on past a paragraph.

If you have multiple issues to explain, you should include them all in the single mandatory-optional essay. Your final length should not go past the 250 words they have suggested. Most people only need a couple sentences to cover each such issue; don't get carried away.

For essay #2, that's noted as "optional" and is asking for any additional information that you want the adcom to know… well that one is more flexible. We're calling that the "optional-optional essay." You can include stuff there that doesn't fit in essay 1 about goals and Wharton, but again, BE SELECTIVE. They really are not asking you to write about just anything here. It should be deployed only with a specific strategy in mind, to cover something concrete.

For any school, your strategy should be to not overstay your welcome. Like a polite and respectful guest, you should enter the Wharton admissions team's domain, offering exactly what they have asked for in their essay prompts and application instructions, and then exit gracefully. It's fine to use this optional-optional essay (Essay 2) if you have something interesting to add *that is not reflected elsewhere in the entire set of application assets.* A similar type of critical thinking as you might use for your Harvard essay could be used here. It's an opportunity. Only take the opportunity if you can add value to the adcom's understanding of who you are. Make it count. Give them something new and useful. Don't just blather on.

One key use of these two optional essays is to screen for emotional intelligence, and decision-making capacity. When faced with vague information, how do you react? Are you able to demonstrate self-awareness and present new information that they can't find elsewhere, that's relevant to your candidacy? If you're saying that you're ready to go be a leader in the business world, and then you submit this wandering morass of an essay under the "optional" heading that has no reason for being, and is just an upchuck of ideas because you think that the adcom needs to experience more of your fine writing abilities in essay form… well, that's not going to score you any points.

If you have something unusual that could affect their impressions of you, that you need them to know about, fine, write a short and sweet essay to cover it. But you should NOT under ANY circumstances feel compelled to write this essay just to fill up space. Your goal is to take up as little of their time as possible in order to convey, with conviction and impact, your main message. Your goal is not to monopolize any more of their mental energy than you absolutely must.

FOR EXAMPLE...

- If you have a gap in your career history, that would be a valid subject to explain in the mandatory-optional essay. OR, if you have a low GPA, that typically also does warrant use of the optional essay, provided that you actually have real information to include, to help the adcom understand what was going on with you during your undergraduate experience. An appropriate mandatory-optional essay on grades might cover items such as working your way through college, or an extreme personal situation like the illness of a family member. That sort of thing. You probably will not be adding value to your candidacy by just saying that you were didn't take school seriously and were partying too much.

- If you've been building a business on the side, and you think it's important to tell the adcom more about it than you can relay in the main essay and your resume, then use the optional-optional essay (Essay 2) to do so. Again, be brief. Cover NEW information that they can't get elsewhere, and make it clear why you're telling them. This makes most sense if you're planning on doing something entrepreneurial in your post-MBA career – but at the same time, we'd imagine that you should be able to cover sufficient info on this in essay 1. So be strategic.

- If you've been actively involved in a community activity that's very important to you and you want to share more of that with the adcom – again, more than you already have on your resume and in the rest of the application dataset – and it's really really an important thing in your life, then maybe that too would work for the optional-optional essay (Essay 2).

- If you were the State Champion Bunjee-Jumper in 2001 and you were training to go on to the Olympics for your sport, but then you got injured and had to sit a season out, and then your parents decided you needed to go to law school, and then you moved around for three years before ending up at college, but then you got into Extreme Frisbee and dropped out of college to pursue that, but then decided to go back finally and now you're working on Wall Street.... then maybe this needs to be covered in the optional-optional essay too (Essay 2). Though truly, if your story is that complicated, then there are other issues that we might be concerned about! But sure, if you have had a non-linear professional history with a lot of different personal pursuits and causes for it to be so jaggedy, you may need the 400 words here to cover it.

- If you're in a band and you currently tour every summer and have a fan base and a couple albums out, and you want to share that with the adcom – that might make sense to include in the optional-optional essay as well (Essay 2). We're doubtful you'd need the full 400 words to do it though.

These are just off-the-cuff examples to help you see what might be appropriate. It's very individual. In most cases, we do not see BSers adding much value in what they write in the optional-optional essay. We encourage you to be strategic in what you're planning on including. Is it bschool-appropriate? Does it share who you are in a way that you cannot do so through the main application assets? Is it additive to your profile? Is it memorable? Will the reader know more about you – in a positive way – after putting down your essay 2? You must answer "yes" to all of those questions before moving forward with the optional-optional essay.

Remember: Do not outstay your welcome! You may think that writing essays is hard, but EssaySnark can tell you, reading them for days on end is absolutely exhausting. Do not submit more to the adcom than they truly need in order to understand who you are and what you're about. Make every bit count.

Reapplicant Essay

As of this writing (June 2014), Wharton's instructions on their Reapplicants page are quite confusing. They say that "All reapplicants to Wharton are required to complete the requisite application essays **plus** the optional essay." *Essays* plural?

What they mean is: Complete the main essay (what will you gain), and complete the reapplicant essay that we've deemed the *mandatory-optional essay* (250 words on how you've improved). If there's still something beyond that that you need to explain, you can also complete the 400-word optional essay (Essay 2).

Someone should really ask Wharton to clarify this on their site. ☺

Anyway, this *SnarkStrategies Guide* is not designed to provide all the advice and guidance that a reapplicant to The Wharton School would need – we actually wrote a whole other book on that (see the EssaySnark Bookstore at essaysnark.com/bookstore for the *Reapplicant Guide*).

To offer everything that *Guide* tells you in a few bullet points:

- You need to show the Wharton adcom how you're a new-and-improved version of yourself this year

- You should focus on content (stories and examples) that happened in the time since you first applied

- Don't re-use stories from your original essays if you can help it.

- It *might* be OK to change your career goals from what you originally pitched, but you need to do so carefully

- The most obvious ways to show improvement are to increase the GMAT (if that was a weakness – if it was already over, say, 700 total, then this may not be a workable strategy) and/or take a class (if the college GPA is a little low).

- Or, if you got a shiny new promotion or move into a completely new role, then that's definitely worth reporting and can often be seen as significant enough for the adcom to admit.

- You should reapply in Round 1 if at all possible.

In the past, Wharton explicitly requested that reapplicants get a new recommendation from their current direct supervisor –yes, even if that person just submitted a rec for you a few months ago when you did your original application. You can use someone else for your reapplicant recommender but you may want to see if your boss would be able to do a new one for you. Just make sure that whoever you choose, that they submit *new* material in their recommendations. Recommendations cannot be reused! You need to leverage this chance to give the adcom an update, and the recommenders are a great place for that to come through.

The current reapplicant page on the Wharton website does not specify one way or another about who they want a rec from (we didn't create an application to check if there are instructions there – it's up to you to review all possible sources of guidance that the school themselves provide so be sure to look at the app itself too). Given that they seem to not be saying one way or another anymore, this may be their way to tell you to use your best judgment.

When you develop your material, it should be additive to what you told them originally – but also, don't force them to pick up last year's essays in order to understand what you're saying. Don't simply say "My career goals are unchanged from last year." Instead, say "Just like I presented last year, my career goals are to do X." Write the essays such that they fit in with what you said last time – or explain the deltas in what's changed – but do so in a way that gives the reader what they need to know here and now, without having to be a detective in researching the different pieces of your puzzle.

Wharton is friendly to reapplicants. They just need to see proof that you're now ready for bschool, that you know why you need the MBA and how you'll use it, and that you'll bring enough from your past experiences that you can contribute effectively in the classroom environment. It is not enough to simply write better essays with clearer sentences and no typos. You need to actually show them why you're a better candidate today than you were last time around.

If you have specific questions on how to tackle a reapplication to Wharton, be sure to stop by the blahg or drop us an email and we'll see what we can do to help.

The Wharton/Lauder Joint Degree

We're not going to go into extensive detail here on what the Lauder program is or the application requirements, but suffice it to say, it's a very intensive joint master's with a focus on languages and international business. Penn Law students can also apply, so you'll be mixed in with people doing other things at the university. It also starts much earlier than the standard MBA, so you'd need to be prepared to get on campus by late spring, and devote your entire summer to the first portion of your Lauder education. It's definitely not the right fit for everyone; it's more work, and you'll be missing out on some bschool activities because your schedule will be overflowing even more than other people's with Lauder-specific stuff.

However, if you want a career overseas, then this is an amazing launch pad for that.

The Lauder program doesn't get that many applicants, so it's actually pretty easy to stand out. You'll be evaluated separately for both Lauder and for the Wharton MBA; if you don't make it into Lauder, you still might get an offer for the MBA track (but not vice versa; you can't make it into Lauder but not Wharton). That being said, admissions officials at Penn have told us in the past that if you apply to a dual-degree program at this university and one department rejects you, you're likely to be rejected by the other. This is certainly not a formal policy or a rule, just a trend to be aware of.

The main difference with a Lauder application is that you'll have a verbal test of your foreign language skills. It's not a big deal if you're reasonably fluent in this non-native language but if you're rusty, then certainly you'll want to study up for it. This interview is done by phone and there are strict timetables when it needs to be completed by. All Lauder applicants must go through this process (it's called OPI, for Oral Proficiency Interview). Check the Lauder website for details.

The Lauder program is more expensive, because it's longer, and because you'll expect to do some international travel, however a little known fact is that there's plenty of funding available for accepted students. We've heard that in almost all cases, those accepted to Lauder are offered some fellowship monies, and we understand the amounts to be at least equivalent to the difference in tuition that you'd be paying from just the standard MBA. So that's a pretty nice perk.

Most Lauder students are international; only about 20% of them are Americans. If you're a U.S. citizen interested in this opportunity, you may have an advantage in the application process. You will be a minority if accepted to the program (that's flipped from what the general MBA population is).

The main advantage in applying to Lauder?

You get a 1,000 word essay to explain why you're interested in it.

Ahhhh. One thousand words. What a luxury, in this day and age of abbreviated essay questions. This is over and above the main essay you'll be writing for the standard MBA app.

Our advice on this?

You don't need to take up all 1,000 words.

We believe that a 750-word essay could be sufficient here. It's completely up to you of course, and if you feel that you have enough compelling content to warrant use of the full space, then by all means, go ahead.

But don't you dare go over.

There are NO EXCUSES for being overlimit on this essay. No they don't count words, but they surely can tell, after reading so many, when someone is going on for longer than typical.

We're not going to offer a whole separate section of advice on constructing the Lauder essay, both because such a small population of Brave Supplicants is truly interested in it, and also because everything that we laid out in discussing the main Wharton essay can also be applied to this task. You need to articulate why this degree is important to you, and how you will make use of the very special opportunity that it represents. It's not the right program for the degree-collector who simply wants to come out with more initials after her name. You need to articulate why this is right for you. This is a process of introspection, research, and reflection – with a keen focus on the goals – just like we laid out in the prior section.

And, obviously, in your Lauder essay, you should explain how your background makes you a good fit for the program. In fact, if you're interested in Lauder, you should reach out to their admissions team and talk about it. They would love for the chance to sell you on what they have, and it's a great way for you to explain why you think it might be a good fit for you – and get their reactions to that.

One bit of advice though: If you're trying for Lauder, then your main Wharton essay should mention that. You don't want to repeat content between the two, but they should be complementary – and you should be upfront about the fact that you're a Lauder candidate. Yes, the adcom reader should be able to see that information from the application dataset that you submit, but it's also such a core part of how you present yourself as a joint degree candidate that it really needs to be mentioned in that essay too. You can still have an international experience in business at Wharton without the Lauder part, so you're not putting your Wharton full-time MBA candidacy at risk for talking about those aspects.

In addition to this separate essay, applicants to Lauder may also be invited to interview. For clarity, what that means is, if your application is strong, then they'll ask you to interview; all accepted applicants are interviewed before admission, but not everyone who applies gets invited to the interview. These Lauder interviews are typically conducted by second-year students who are in the Lauder program, or alumni of it; sometimes Lauder staff do them when there's lack of availability in your part of the world. Wherever possible, these interviews are done in conjunction with your MBA interview (another reason to come on campus for the Team-Based Discussion if you can).

If you end up as a reapplicant to Lauder then contact them before working on your strategy. The Lauder Institute folks are very approachable and encouraging. They won't necessarily give you feedback on what you did wrong the first time out, but since the main reason for someone being rejected is that it wasn't clear why the Lauder option is the right fit, then having a conversation with Lauder admissions will help you clarify your goals and interests and give you insights on whether those are in line with what this program can offer.

For that matter, anyone interested in Lauder should contact them. We mentioned that above but it's really the best advice possible. We often suggest that applicants reach out to the schools to discuss their interests and goals but in the case of a potential Lauder candidate, then it's a complete no-brainer. You'll want to leverage all resources available, and this admissions team is one of the most open and inviting around. They want to talk to you. Make the most of that.

The Wharton Team-Based Discussion and Your Interview

Wharton introduced what at the time was a fairly radical innovation a few years back, with its Team-Based Discussion group interview format. This was rolled out as a standard part of admissions in Fall 2012. Some say that the group discussion contributed to some application volume declines but we have a hard time believing that. We never once heard someone say they were reluctant to apply to Wharton because of a group interview. You do still have a one-on-one interview at Wharton, but it's very short – often about 15 minutes – and it's generally conducted with a second-year student. If you're applying to Lauder or the HCM, then your interview experience will be more extensive.

The bulk of the MBA "interview" experience is this Team-Based Discussion, which is a small-group exercise you'll complete with other short-listed candidates. They're calling this a "team discussion" but it's hard to fully agree with the "team" characterization – how can you be a "team" when it's a group of complete strangers you will have only met for the very first time that day? Team dynamics take time to develop. We think this should more accurately be called a *group assessment*.

Whatever.

The Wharton group interview format isn't exactly new; IESE in Spain started doing group evaluations a few years ago with their applicants from India, and has since expanded it to all candidates they're serious considering. Among U.S. bschools, yes, the Wharton format is indeed innovative.

We saw Wharton start experimenting with the interview process in 2011. For years and years, interviews were all done the same: You got your interview invite, and you got hooked up with a Wharton alum in your city, who conducted the interview with you and then reported her findings back to admissions. Many schools still do things this way. It's efficient in terms of time and resources, particularly with such big schools like Columbia and Kellogg that interview a lot of candidates.

The downsides to this though were quality control – the admissions office often is unable to do much training nor do they have much oversight over their alums. It creates a nonstandard experience for the candidates and the post-interview reports have a lot of variability. Wharton first tried to counter that by integrating standard questions into their interviews and changing them frequently, but that didn't work – immediately after they interview, lots of candidates run straight to their computers to post about their experiences, and the questions they were asked, on the applicant forums.

Then in 2011, Wharton made a big step of pulling in their interviews. They took the task off the shoulders of their alumni and instead moved to a more closely-managed process where only adcom members and current students did them. We thought that was a great move; we've long felt that alumni are not the best interviewers unless the process is managed very carefully, as it's done at London Business School, for example. We were happy to see Wharton relieve their alum from these interviewing duties. (Sometimes Lauder alumni still perform interviews for that program but it's more unusual.)

Since then, Wharton did even more to renovate the process. The Team-Based Discussion is useful as it allows the adcom to observe candidates in action. Wharton still has one-on-one sessions where you meet with an interviewer privately, but these have been reported to be quite informally (especially when compared to the intensity of some school's one-on-one interviews). EssaySnark thinks that Wharton is only including them in the process in order to pre-empt all the complaints they'd receive from short-listed candidates who didn't end up with an offer. We can just hear it – the applicant goes through all the steps and gets spit out the other end but never had an actual interview. They call up Admissions in a huff, feeling that they'd been short-changed. "All the other schools interviewed me!" they exclaim. "Why didn't you?" They would blame the lack of an interview experience as the reason they were rejected. Separate observation: The schools that offer applicant-initiated interviews – Duke, Tuck and Kellogg – are the ones that applicants report feeling the most positive about during their admissions process. The inverse is surely the case, too.

We're being a bit cynical here. Yes, the one-on-one meeting with a second-year does give you a nice chance for an interaction with another member of the Wharton community, and it gives them another few datapoints to evaluate your candidacy by. But how much are they going to learn about you in that format?

From the reports of others who've gone before, it appears that many of those interviews have been more "Tell me what you want to know about Wharton" - where the student interviewer lays it open for the candidate to guide the conversation.

(The interviewer could still get plenty of insights about the candidate with this technique – don't be fooled into thinking that they wouldn't.)

The bulk of your post-essay evaluation comes out in the group experience. So let's walk through what that's about – with the understanding that this information is based on how they did it last year, and these things do tend to get tweaked from season to season, so what Wharton does with you and the Team Based Discussion invite may be somewhat different this year.

Where are interviews held

When they invite you to interview, the admissions office will provide some information on how it works and what to expect when the interview invitation comes along. The logistical complexities of organizing these group experiences in specific locations around the world obviously is one impetus behind their new encouragement of early applications – if they get your app in hand sooner, then they have a better idea of how many people they need to accommodate around the world.

Before you begin to freak out: No, they do not require anyone to travel to campus for this interview experience – though if you can do so, EssaySnark strongly recommends it. In fact, *Wharton* recommends it – check out the Interviews section on their website for exactly that suggestion. It will not negatively affect your chances if you cannot go to Philadelphia for the interview, but there are certainly benefits to you if you can, and it would be impressive if you came from an exceptionally far distance to do so.

It's OK if you can't pull this off. Wharton will be offering interviews in select cities around the world. So, unless you are in some insanely distant locale where you're the only candidate within 3,000 square miles (as in, you're currently in the service on active deployment), the admissions team will be able to collect a group of you together to ~~put through the wringer~~ conduct the team exercises with. Wharton admissions does significant travel to accommodate the far-flung population of applicants. The HBS Admissions Board has long done this type of traveling for interviews, too – they must rack up a lot of frequent flier miles along the way!!

Note that you *may* have to travel within your region, however – and you should be prepared to do so. **Don't even apply if you won't be able to pull this off.** Financial constraints are *not* a good reason to state to the adcom for why you can't come meet them wherever they might want you to. Remember, you're applying for a big-ticket purchase; if you cannot pull off the minimal expense of a train or plane ticket to get to the city where the adcom is hosting these interview events, then it's honestly not a very positive indication to the adcom that you can afford a top-shelf MBA.

Typically this might mean traveling to Delhi when you live in India, for example – though note that sometimes schools have to cast a wider net. If you're in India, you may want to be mentally prepared to go as far as, say, Dubai for your interview. This is unlikely to be required of the Wharton admissions process, though in past years, Harvard has had fewer international interview sites for their Round 1 candidates and that was how they arranged things – just so you know.

How it works

In the 2013-2014 admissions season, Wharton would issue interview invitations on a specific day of the week, in a batch, once a week for three or four weeks.

In Round 1 2014, they consolidated to a big-bang approach: Everyone they wanted to interview in Round 1 would get the invite on a single day (in this case, it was Friday, October 31st) and if they knew they didn't want to move forward with you, you were released on that day. They then held interviews (or, Team Based Discussions) at different locations around the world during a very short window in the middle of November.

In past years, when you got the invite, you'd be informed of several possible questions that you may be asked to discuss with your group. You wouldn't know which question they're going to give to you until you begin the actual exercise. You will need to research all of these different topics in advance – but the admissions team asks that you not spend too much time on research. They recommend just an hour total.

At the time of your Team-Based Discussion, you'll be assigned to a small group of candidates. You can expect all of them to be dissimilar to you – the admissions team constructs these groups carefully. You may have one or two people in your group for whom English is their second language (or you may be that person). You may have a finance type and a consulting type and a marketing type – and a teacher, or an ex-Marine, or someone else from a very non-traditional background. You will have people from all over the world in your group. Watching how you navigate the group dynamics are an important part of the exercise.

The actual exercise takes about 45 minutes. They set you up with the instructions at the beginning: They tell you which of the topics your group has, and you'll be given 30 minutes or so to discuss it with the group, and then you will need to present your recommendations and conclusions on that topic.

The admissions folks will completely step aside after laying out the instructions, and will be silent observers (and active note-takers!). It's up to you to present your ideas to the group, get buy-in if you feel yours are the best, or debate, discuss, and compromise with the others.

Remember that everyone will come in prepared with how they think the presentation should be made. They will all have their own ideas – and as a group, bschool students are assertive. At least, as a general rule they are. You should not expect your ideas to be adopted readily by everyone else, when they have their own ideas that they want to sell.

We're not going to tell you how to handle this since obviously all your background, professional experience, and training in different contexts are what will carry you through.

We will show you one of the topics they used in the past, since they don't seem to be reusing them from round to round:

> For this discussion, we would like you to imagine that the following question has been posed to your team:
>
> At The Wharton School, our mission is to generate knowledge that transforms global business and advances society. As a foundation to support the creation of knowledge and translation to action, Thomas Robertson, Dean of The Wharton School outlined a strategic foundation for the School, represented by the "Three Pillars" of Innovation, Global Presence and Social Impact. To learn more, you can watch Dean Robertson describe the Three Pillars here,
> http://www.youtube.com/watch?v=5lCsAHtJV0Q
>
> **Wharton School Dean Thomas S. Robertson Outlines a Vision for Growth**
>
> Imagine that as potential future Wharton MBA students, you have been asked by Dean Robertson to provide your recommendations regarding a $1 million USD gift that a recent alumna has given to the school. Her singular criterion is that the money is invested in one of the Three Pillars. How would you and your team choose to invest this money and why?

That was just one of at least six possible topics they used for candidates in 2012. They switched the questions between Round 1 and Round 2 (and probably Round 3 – we don't know 'cuz we didn't have any BSers trying then). It wouldn't hurt for you to spend some time ruminating on that question even if it won't be used in the TBD this year. What you come up with could be relevant to the entirety of your app. And if you're very curious, it's easy enough, once the first batch is through, to use a little bit of Google to uncover the questions that are being presented to TBDers in the current admissions season.

How to prepare

You definitely want to work out some possibilities in advance of the Team-Based Discussion. You're going to be nervous going into it. You want to have something at the ready. It will likely be harder to come up with something brilliant on the spot than it would be to walk into the room with some content on deck.

Snarky Strategy #5

Prepare at least two ideas for each topic they send you.

When you get sent your own list of topics for your Team-Based Discussion, then our best advice is to prepare at least two different ideas in response to each of the choices that they lay out. In a team discussion, it's likely that someone else will present the same ideas as you had before you get a chance to mention them. You want to have something unique to contribute to the conversation even if you're the last one to get to speak.

Also, don't be too attached to your ideas. This evaluation is NOT grading you on the ideas; the admissions team cares a lot more about how you interact with your peers. That doesn't mean that you should be passive – just be cautious about coming across as too aggressive, too. A mature and composed applicant will be able to navigate the give-and-take of ideas in a way that lets him or her make appropriate contributions at the right time, without monopolizing the conversation, and while allowing others' voices to be heard. If you find yourself in a quieter group, which does sometimes happen, then it might be appropriate for you to take a more proactive role in guiding the discussion and moving people towards consensus, if that's your style – but tread carefully, and don't jostle.

When you prepare your ideas, you may want to keep your own application pitch in mind. Having your possible responses line up with what you wrote in your essays is always a good idea. You may want to cross-reference the stuff you think of for your TBD topics against the essays themselves. By the time you go for the interview and team discussion, your essays will be a distant memory, so pull those back up on your computer screen and read over what you wrote. If you need to, then it's OK for your TBD topics to be unrelated to the essay content – but if you can make a personal connection of some sort between the two, then that might be an extra bonus.

That being said: It's unlikely that these connections will actually make their way back to notes in your application file, but it's possible that they will depending on how you present them or what your contributions to the conversation end up being. Don't be obnoxious and say, "Well, as I talked about in my essays, blah blah blah." The TBD is about working with a group of your peers. Forget the fact that you're being observed; don't "play to the audience" in that way. Pandering like that could really backfire.

You should still prepare your standard interview material for Wharton just as you'd do for any other top bschool, because you'll have some one-on-one time with an admissions person (or student) as part of this experience. Even if you just were to meet an admissions person at an info session, it helps to know why you want an MBA. You want to be prepared for all instances – even just standing in line waiting for coffee during the break. You don't want to be the deer in headlights when they ask you the basic questions like, "So, tell me.... Why do you want to come to The Wharton School?"

Interview prep advice is beyond scope of this essay guide, and it's too far in the distance for you to be worrying about now anyway, if you haven't even started your essays. Well-written essays are the first step and are the obvious prerequisite to seeing that interview invite come through, so get started on that and take the interview process when it comes.

What to Do Next

This is not meant as an end-all, be-all guide on all things Wharton. In fact, if you REALLY want to go to this school, you'd do yourself a favor by going to Philly and actually visit the place. Check out the campus. Sit in on a class. Ask questions. Go to South Street and see what the nightlife is like. Meet people. Learn about them.

No, Wharton will deny your app just because you didn't visit campus, but truly, it can make a big difference in knowing what the school is about and knowing whether it's the right place for you (plus it'll give you additional ammo to put into these all-important essays).

Want more help? Swing by the EssaySnark blahg at http://essaysnark.com to ask a question, or drop the team an email at gethelpnow@essaysnark.com to inquire about our specialized MBA consulting services for Wharton and all the other top bschools in the world.

Follow EssaySnark on Twitter!

https://twitter.com/EssaySnark

www.ingramcontent.com/pod-product-compliance
Lightning Source LLC
Chambersburg PA
CBHW081842170426
43199CB00017B/2818